Gardening with Colour

Creative Design Ideas for Canadian Gardens

Rob Sproule

Lone Pine Publishing

Lone Pine Publishing
10145 – 81 Avenue
Edmonton, AB T6E 1W9
Canada
Website: www.lonepinepublishing.com

Library and Archives Canada Cataloguing in Publication

Sproule, Rob, 1978-
        Gardening with colour : creative design ideas for Canadian gardens / Rob Sproule.

Includes index.
ISBN 978-1-55105-873-3

        1. Color in gardening. 2. Plants, Ornamental--Color.
3. Gardens--Design. I. Title.

SB454.3.C64S67 2011   635.9'68   C2010-906917-X

Editorial Director: Nancy Foulds
Project Editor: Sheila Quinlan
Production Manager: Gene Longson
Layout and Production: Janina Kuerschner
Cover Design: Gerry Dotto

Photo Credits: All photos are by Rob Sproule except: Ball Seed Company 234; Anne Brown 32; Mark Burleton 175, 257a; Con Boland Photography 67; Tamara Eder 312c; Maureen Elhatton 64; Yvonne Glass 9; Carrie Hamilton 47, 233a, 299; Liz Hull 223; Gail Lacey 53b; Wilf Maul 38, 69b; Curtis Morie 18, 33; Megan Mundell 7, 15, 19a, 21, 23, 27b, 40, 49b, 51, 54, 59, 69a, 73, 77b, 80f, 89c, 90, 92b, 104f, 105, 110, 111, 112a, 118, 120c, 122, 123, 126, 139, 141b, 145a, 149, 153a&b, 155, 160c, 164b, 171, 173, 174, 176d, 177b, 193, 198, 201a, 209a, 215, 217a, 221a, 229a, 232b, 237a, 238, 240d&f, 242, 246, 249a, 250, 253, 256b, 257b, 260d, 261, 267, 269a, 275, 278, 279all, 280c&d, 281, 303, 304a, 305a&c, 307, 320; Renee Oswald 12, 301b; Allison Penko 100c, 160b; Laura Peters 104e, 116d, 120g, 268c&d; photos.com 108e; Vera Popnik 225; Proven Winners 1, 45, 52, 65, 66, 76a, 84a, 88b&c, 104c, 112b&d, 116b&c, 120b,d&f, 124c&d, 125, 128c, 132b&d, 133, 140c, 144c, 145b, 148a&b, 150, 152a,b,e&f, 154, 156a&c, 160a, 167, 168b, 170, 172b&c, 181b, 184a,b&d, 187, 188c&d, 189a&b, 191, 192c&e, 196c, 200d, 202, 203, 204a&b, 205a&b, 208b&c, 210, 212all, 213, 214, 216all, 220e, 222, 224b&d, 226, 227, 228a,b,c&d, 229b, 232d&e, 240b, 243, 244b, 248b, 251, 252a,b&c, 258, 259, 260a&b, 262, 264all, 268b, 272c, 280b, 284c, 285, 290, 291, 292b, 293, 294, 296a&b, 297a&b, 300a&c; Kim Sokil 55; Unknown 6.

Design Credits: Ball Seed Company 234; Butchart Gardens 98, 134, 166, 174, 198, 218, 270; Hole's Greenhouses 78, 302; Val MacMillan 146; Minter Gardens 138, 158, 274, 310; Cynthia Mundell 282; Megan Mundell 190; Original Joe's Restaurant 86; Proven Winners 150, 154, 170, 202, 210, 214, 222, 226, 258, 262, 290, 294; Mario Salazar 102; Salisbury Greenhouse 82, 90, 94, 106, 110, 122, 126, 130, 162, 182, 206, 254; Southlands Nursery 278, 286, 298, 306; Rob Sproule 74, 178, 186, 194, 230; Unknown 114, 118, 142; Wellington Garden Centre 238, 242, 246, 250, 266.

We acknowledge the financial support of the Government of Canada through the Canada Book Fund (CBF) for our publishing activities.

PC: 15

Contents

Dedication

To Meg, for inspiring and challenging me every day to be a better artist. This book wouldn't have happened without you.

Acknowledgements

First and foremost, thanks to Meg for being the brains behind the project, for putting up with me over the many months it took to write it, for taking endless pictures with me, and for having the perseverance of a consistent vision. A giant thanks to my whole family, especially my mom, who have all been tremendously supportive. You are the most important people in my life and I thank you all so much.

Thanks to my business partners for giving me the time I needed to write this. I am blessed to be working alongside my family. Thank you to the entire staff at Salisbury Greenhouse for being supportive and enthusiastic, and thanks especially to Anna Pandos, Mario Salazar, Tanya Smith and our container design team for contributing pictures or designs. Thanks of course to the entire team at Lone Pine for believing in me and giving me creative freedom for this project. I also want to thank Bert Almon for giving me time off from my thesis; I couldn't have asked for a better teacher.

This was a complex book and a lot of people contributed in making it a reality, whether that was in answering questions, allowing me to use pictures from their establishments or sending pictures of their container gardens from across Canada. Their support was invaluable, and it's thanks to them that I was able to include such a wide range of design styles.

On the next page I list the contact information of the businesses that helped me the most on this book. In addition, thanks to Proven Winners (www.provenwinners.com) for allowing the use of your photos and for the remarkable container designs you bring to the gardening world. Thanks as well to Ball Seed Company, the Muttart Conservatory, Con Boland Photography, Earl's Restaurants, the Manor Cafe, the Hotel MacDonald, the City of Edmonton, In Bloom Custom Container Planting in Edmonton, the City of Victoria, the City of Quebec and Premier Tech.

To everyone else who opened their front and back yards to Meg and me, thank you! It wouldn't have been the same book without pictures from the yards of Val MacMillan, Cindy Mundell, Lynn Parker, Luella Chmelyk, Sharon Adams, Donna and Mario Salazar, Con Boland and Cheryl Williams. A special thanks to Mark Burleton of Rideau Hall for your support and to Linda Mundell for hosting us in Vancouver.

Thanks to Pat Brehaut for spreading the word to the gardening community with the Edmonton Horticultural Society (through President Jan Ogilvie) and the Strathcona in Bloom Society (through President Cliff Lacey). Thank you to everyone who submitted their photos. I was blown away by how many amazing yards and containers I was sent. A special thanks to Anne Brown, Bryan Doidge, Maureen Elhatton, Yvonne Glass, Carrie Hamilton, Liz Hull, Gail Lacey, Wilf Maul, Renee Oswald, Vera Popnik and Kim Sokil, whose yards are represented in the book.

Recommended Businesses

In order to make this book truly Canadian, I travelled west and worked with friends to the east to find as broad a sample of remarkable containers as possible. Below is a list of the show gardens, garden centres and nurseries that I recommend as some of the best locations in the country to go to find innovative plant designs and container gardens. If you're in the area of any of them, I highly recommend that you stop by and let them inspire you!

My greenhouse—and I'd love for you to visit!

Salisbury Greenhouse
Range Road 232
Sherwood Park, Alberta
780-467-5743
www.salisburygreenhouse.com

Others, from east to west:

Plant World Garden Centre
4000 Eglinton Avenue West
Etobicoke, Ontario
416-241-9174
www.plantworld.net

Shelmerdine Garden Centre
7800 Roblin Boulevard
Winnipeg, Manitoba
204-895-7203
www.shelmerdine.com

Dutch Growers
3320 Pasqua Street
Regina, Saskatchewan
306-721-GROW
www.dutchgrowers.net

Wellington Garden Centre
13648 142 Street
Edmonton, Alberta
780-455-2281
www.wellingtongardencentre.com

Minter Gardens
52892 Bunker Road
Rosedale, British Columbia
1-888-MINTERS
www.mintergardens.com

Southlands Nursery
6550 Balaclava Street
Vancouver, British Columbia
604-261-6411
www.southlandsnursery.com

The Butchart Gardens
800 Benvenuto Avenue
Brentwood Bay, British Columbia
866-652-4422
www.butchartgardens.com

Introduction

I CONSIDER MYSELF lucky to have two great passions in my life. The first is plants, for which I have an ongoing fascination that keeps me intrigued, surprised and smiling every morning on my way to work. The second is poetry and the written word. I've been addicted to writing and reading my whole life, but it wasn't until I met my wife Meg, who is a gifted and inspiring visual artist, that I began to recognize the intersections between written and visual art. The more I thought about visual art and began to learn about some of the design principles it used, the more I realized that container gardening used the same principles. I realized that container gardening is a type of sculpture.

This book is about how easy it is to use plants to make living art. Using living things to make a living, breathing, changing sculpture is an elegant creative outlet, and your living, changing compositions will be especially dynamic if you keep in mind some simple principles of design. The design principles are universal laws that you can use to make your containers beautiful and catch the eye of everyone who visits your garden. They are easy to learn and, once you know them, you'll start to think of your designs as art, your garden as the gallery, and yourself as the artist who makes it all happen.

I have two goals with this book: I want to give you the tools you need to make you confident enough to be creative

Salisbury Greenhouse from the air, just east of Edmonton, Alberta

and take chances with your own living art; and I want to make you excited about gardening. It's truly an art form with no boundaries. Whatever your space, budget or time limitations are, you always have as many possibilities at your fingertips as your inspiration allows. I hope this book gives you enough ideas that it gets your creativity flowing, and enough confidence in designing that it makes you bold enough to create containers that are true expressions of yourself.

A History of Garden Design

If we follow the history of gardening all the way back, it would take us to the first people who deliberately decided to plant seeds in the ground instead of foraging. The history of design in gardening, however, starts quite a bit later. It wasn't until humans developed cities and a leisure class that they began to think about gardening for pleasure instead of strictly for utility. Using the principles of design to lay out plantings and gardens in appealing ways followed shortly after.

Many of the first large kingdoms and great cities were in the deserts of Persia, Babylon and Egypt. The leisure class of these kingdoms developed elaborate irrigation techniques so that they could grow lavish, moisture-loving plants to create humid, living oases in defiance of the deserts of modern-day Iran, Iraq and Egypt. Just as Canadian gardens are often full of tropical species of annuals, usually needing special care and extra water, these ancient gardens were elaborate and decadent. A dignitary from another kingdom, having travelled across deserts to get to one of these cities, would have been astonished and impressed at the power of that city when he walked into a tropical garden overflowing with life.

Canada has many different climatic zones. This stunning magnolia tree from Niagara-on-the-Lake isn't hardy in many other parts of the country.

The most famous example of one of these gardens is, of course, the fabled Hanging Gardens of Babylon. The legend is that King Nebuchadnezzar, who took power in 605 BCE, built the gardens to cheer up his homesick bride, Amyitis, who had come from the green, rolling mountains of Persia to Babylon, on the baked desert of the Mesopotamian plateau (close to modern-day Baghdad), as part of a political arrangement. The gardens were irrigated by the Euphrates River using an elaborate irrigation system (and a lot of slaves).

Garden design took a step backward for a few hundred years after the fall of the Roman Empire and the decay of Rome's decadent gardens. Throughout the Middle Ages, gardens were mostly created by monks who grew herbs and, occasionally, flowers within their high monastery walls.

During the Renaissance, wealthy people began to keep their own gardens within their private spaces, but it wasn't until the 17th and 18th centuries that garden design began to mature as an art form. The bafflingly decadent gardens of continental Europe not only infuriated whole populations to the point of revolution but also pioneered many of the methods of gardening that are popular today.

In Canada, gardening for most people meant planting rows of vegetables—until the explosion of suburban homes after World War II. In the decades following, container design took a backseat to the ubiquitous flower beds of geraniums and marigolds that lined every manicured suburban street. It wasn't until big companies such as Proven Winners started introducing high-performance

Be creative with your containers!
Here are some gorgeous window boxes over a cafe in Quebec City.

annuals in the mid-1990s that container gardening really came into its own. The recent explosion of interest in container design is phenomenal, and for gardeners today the sky is the limit for how creative and imaginative they can be in their gardens.

The Layout of this Book

This book is centred around the elements and principles of design: simple, universal rules for what looks good and what doesn't. They can be applied to all visual arts, including gardening. I want to give you ideas and inspiration to make your own designs and guide you on how to add the elements of design to your gardening tool box so you can use them effectively in your own garden. The section beginning on page 40 will acquaint you with these basic rules and begin to show you how to use them in your designs.

There are 60 feature designs in the book, each with a diagram, a list of ingredients and care instructions. For each one I discuss what elements of design the container uses most effectively. You can imitate the feature recipes, but please feel free to use the basic design and substitute as widely as you like. It's your garden, after all, and as the artist you make the rules about what fits in your outdoor space. The designs in the book are meant as guidelines, inspiring starting points from where you can begin. With each design I try to give you tips for how to take the initial design and run with it, including variations and suggestions for what to use as substitutes within the container while still keeping the general essence of the design.

I want to emphasize that you don't need to follow these designs exactly. If you're just starting out and are looking for some proven designs then by all means follow the diagrams, but I encourage you to be creative and take some risks; if it doesn't work you

Every garden should have a peaceful sitting area where you can go to unwind at the end of a stressful day and let the plants nurture you.

can start over next year. I've included the basic care requirements for most of the plants in the book so that you can feel more comfortable using substitutions. As long as you think about those requirements while substituting (i.e., don't put full sun plants in a full shade container), you'll be fine. The designs in this book are meant to inspire!

The Top Five Questions

Garden centres are the front lines of the rapidly changing world of gardening, where beginners and experts alike come to browse, mingle and chat about their ideas and inspirations. It's through my daily conversations with gardeners that I learn which plants, colours and trends have the most buzz and which ones are "so last season." All those conversations and questions have also taught me that the majority of the questions about plants, from "what can I put in a hot, dry location" to "will these two plants go well together," can be summed up in the five categories that follow. My goal is to answer these questions for you right off the bat for each design and ingredient so that you can move on to the really important part of getting creative with them.

Question 1: Size and Habit

Height and spread of plants will vary with region, but I've provided a range for each design as an estimate of how much space and the size of container you'll need. Regions that receive cold nights into June may not see their plants grow to the same size as warmer regions. Size also depends on the variety and can often range dramatically. When choosing your plants, it's important to think about shape as well as size, especially if you're choosing plants to incorporate into a design. In a container there are usually three central elements.

Centrepiece plants provide the vertical focal point and are often the most striking architectural feature. Their shape ranges from very vertical (millet, cleome) to more loosely vertical and airy (gaura, purple fountain grass) to lush, leafy and just plain large (canna lily, hibiscus). The shape of your centrepiece plant will usually determine the shape of your container garden, so it's important to look at the habit of the plant in addition to the numeric height and spread.

Shrubs make excellent centrepieces, and as a bonus you can plant them in the garden in fall. If you're thinking of adding a shrub to your yard, you can get a free container centrepiece out of the deal.

Central plants (fillers) are the flowering or foliage plants that will provide the body and the bulk of your container. They typically have a mounding habit. When you're choosing them, keep in mind the proportion

These hanging baskets have just been hung and are growing for the spring season at Salisbury.

of their size to the size of the rest of the elements in the container.

Trailing plants are cascading plants that flow out of the container and provide a sense of height to the container garden and soften the container itself. Some trailing plants, such as calibrachoa, have a lot of volume and may compete with your filler plants for space; you might want to leave some room for them to grow upward as well as down. Others, such as bacopa, will tend to trail right away.

Keeping shape and habit, as well as height and spread, in mind while you're choosing plants will help you to choose plants that fit neatly into your vision.

Question 2: Exposure

Plants can't go and find shade if they're too hot. They're stuck where we plant them, and because for most annuals our gardens are a long, long way from their original homeland, we have to approximate where they want to be. I think of a garden centre as a United Nations of plants. The plants you browse through in spring have been pulled from the four corners of the earth, and a plant native to the deep jungles of Colombia might be on the bench beside one from the Namibian desert (and their journey from there to the garden centre is usually fascinating). A plant will thrive most if it's planted in a spot that mimics the conditions of the region where it has evolved and grown for thousands of years. If you have a fiery south exposure then you might decide on a plant from the open Australian scrub-land, or if your yard is sunny but the light is dappled under trees, then you might want to choose a European woodland plant.

Exposed sunny spots are perfect for rock gardens and can be gorgeous in the summer heat.

Shady nooks can be some of the most relaxing places in the yard.

I will often make caveats in the book for different exposure levels in different parts of the country. Canada is a massive country with many climatic regions. The most important factor for our purposes is the intensity of the sunlight. Although more humid areas of the country, namely those near the coast and as far inland as southern Ontario in the east and central British Columbia in the west, can get very hot, the high humidity tempers the sun's intensity so that plants can handle more exposure. Plants that love humidity, such as begonias and impatiens, love these humid areas. The geographic centre of Canada, namely the Prairies and the Northwest Territories, are cooler but drier, so the sun is very intense. Some plants that thrive in full sun in humid regions will potentially wilt or burn in full sun on the prairies. I will warn you if full exposure plants are not suitable for dry heat.

Each design and each plant will get one, or sometimes two, of three symbols.

A full sun indicates that the plants need at least six hours of good sunlight to perform at their best. Less sunlight will probably start to cause their original compact, pleasing habit to get leggy and their foliage to turn a paler shade of green. Many full-sun plants are also drought-tolerant plants that have adapted to arid conditions. These plants are ideal for your south-facing deck or patio, under the white siding that reflects the sun.

A sun with cloud indicates that the plants still need a good amount of sun but will have to be protected from the afternoon sun. Exposure to morning sun is perfect for these plants, but they will typically also be good in dappled afternoon sun (for example, south exposure but sheltered by large trees) or evening sun.

Clouds indicate that the plants need to be sheltered. These plants often come from tropical regions where very little sunlight filters down to the jungle floor. These plants are typically good for areas that receive partial sun, but they can tolerate less. All plants love sun; it's the intensity of the sun that they need to be sheltered from. In Miami, New Guinea impatiens grow in full southern exposures, but the humidity there is extremely high. Ultimately it's trial and error to see what will grow best in the different spots of your yard.

Question 3: Moisture

The amount of water a plant gets is arguably the most determining factor of its development. As with sunlight, the amount of water a plant needs is largely a product of its native land. Root systems evolve in response to the amount of water that is available,

and if a plant gets a dramatically different amount of water than what it needs or is accustomed to over a sustained period, the roots won't be able to properly deal with it and the plant will suffer.

Most of the annuals we sell at the greenhouse are destined to be planted in containers, usually with other annuals. Because a container is a closed space, there's less room for error than there is in the ground. Containers dry out faster, so if you don't have much time to spend in the garden and want containers that are low maintenance, then you won't want to pack high-moisture plants tightly together into a small pot or you'll have to water them all the time. If you want to incorporate many different types of plants into the garden, then you'll want to match plants that have similar moisture requirements in each container. For example, bacopa (high moisture) should not be planted with succulents (low moisture), or it will be very hard to keep both of them healthy.

The droplet symbol is designed to tell you how much water your plant needs to perform at its best. Telling you the amount of water a plant needs isn't just for its well-being, but for yours as well. Watering is a time-consuming aspect of gardening, and while some people find it to be a relaxing end to a day at the office, others see it as a chore, and though they may love their garden, they want to do as little work in it as possible. If you do plant high-moisture or high-performance plants (like trailing petunias), you will need to water them more often. However, these are often the plants that really put the "wow" factor into your garden, providing the lush tropical leaves and the avalanches of flowers that provide the finishing touches.

One drop means that the plants are drought tolerant and are likely to appreciate sandy, very well-draining soils. These plants have often evolved in arid regions and often have small, fragile root systems because they have come to rely on small amounts of surface water. Drought-tolerant plants don't like to be plunked into large containers; often the pot you buy it in will suffice for the season. If you

do transplant it into a large container, make sure the medium drains freely. Allow the surface of the soil to dry visibly between waterings, but remember that it's not healthy for any plant to wilt. If you plant in a peat moss–based mix, water it when the medium pulls slightly away from the sides of the container, indicating that the spongy peat fibres are drying up. Always water until the water flows from the bottom of the container to make sure all the soil is moistened. If you've let it get bone dry, you may have to water it twice. If you have a saucer under the plant, make sure to empty it of run-off or rain water. Arid-loving plants universally hate wet feet, and their roots rot easily. These are good plants to get if you're going to be away a lot of the summer.

Succulents are ideal for hot, dry areas and will grow happily in sandy soils. They are also one of the trendiest things on the market.

For areas of the garden that never dry out, plant marginals, which are basically marsh plants and are happiest when they never dry out.

Two drops mean that the plants like their moisture level just right. I still recommend a freely-draining medium and an empty saucer (or no saucer at all) underneath. When the surface begins to dry, poke your finger into the soil. If it's dry to the first knuckle, it's time to water.

Three drops mean that the plants need to be kept consistently moist. They are often tropical or marginal in origin. When the surface of the soil is beginning to dry out, water it. If you want to take an extra step to ensure their health, put a layer of cedar mulch on the soil in your container. Mulch isn't just for perennial and shrub beds; in a container it prevents evaporation and looks and smells wonderful.

Just because a plant needs a lot of water doesn't mean that it can be planted in muddy soil that doesn't drain very well, or in a pot with no holes. Lots of water doesn't mean stagnant water. Plant roots pull oxygen out of the water just like fish gills and will deoxygenate stagnant water until the plant drowns in it. At Salisbury we plant all of our plants, no matter their moisture requirements, in the same very well-draining medium; the difference is in the amount we water.

Question 4: Fertilizer

Fertilizers are big business, and as such gardeners are inundated with commercials, hype and hyperbole about the latest holy water that they just can't do without. Most of the annuals being introduced every year (especially those with the most publicity) are very high feeders. They are like race cars that need high-octane fuel; they have been bred to grow in an unsustainable sprint, exhausting themselves by the end of the season, and they need supplements to do it.

Other groups of plants, like shrubs, perennials and houseplants, which are also gorgeous in container design, usually don't need the same amount of fertilizer as the hyped-up annuals do.

There are two groups of fertilizers: organic and inorganic. Each group has its advantages and disadvantages. Before you believe the next commercial you see, let's cut through the hype and get down to the basics.

Inorganic fertilizers are the N-P-K fertilizers, most commonly the water solubles that turn your water a light blue. In the short term, inorganics are the most potent fertilizers, but they are also becoming increasingly controversial. There are many brands, but they are all combinations of three basic elements: nitrogen (N), phosphorus (P) and potassium (K).

The numbers on the label represent the percentage of the element in the fertilizer; the higher the number, the more punch that particular element is packing. The numbers rarely add up to 100 percent; the rest is filler.

If you're wondering what the different combinations do, the answer is, "top, down, all-around." Nitrogen (top) promotes healthy foliage and leaf growth. If your plant isn't getting enough nitrogen, the leaves turn pale and become sickly looking. However, if it's getting too much nitrogen (i.e., if you fertilize your petunias with 30-10-10), you'll get a beautiful plant that looks a lot like lettuce but has few flowers. Phosphorus (down) stimulates the roots. Fertilizers with a high middle number are like espresso shots to freshly planted annuals and perennials, jump-starting the roots into vigorous growth. A 15-30-15 fertilizer will keep flowering plants blooming. Potassium (all-around)

Inorganic fertilizers are colourful and work very quickly, but those with high numbers come with a hidden environmental price tag.

is the least understood but, in my opinion, the most important of the three elements. It's like a multivitamin for plants. It contains micronutrients such as iron, zinc, copper, sulphur and others that, just like us, plants need in very small amounts. The best all-around inorganic fertilizer is 20-20-20 because of its high last number. Think of 20-20-20 as a balanced diet, whereas others such as 10-52-10 are high calorie, short-term diets. I recommend 20-20-20 to keep annuals healthy all season.

The biggest drawbacks of inorganic fertilizers are that they are a short-term fix and that, because you apply them via watering, a considerable amount spills out and flows into the water table. If you plant something with a small root mass and douse it with a watering can full of 10-52-10, the tiny root system is only going to catch a tiny fraction of the phosphorus. The waste is making inorganics increasingly unpopular among environmentally aware gardeners. Excess inorganic fertilizer finds its way into rivers, lakes and eventually oceans, and along the way, the high amounts of nitrates and phosphates are gobbled up by algae, allowing it to grow exponentially. Massive algal blooms consume all available oxygen in a lake or pond, starving aquatic plants and fish of oxygen and life. The result is a eutrophic water body, wherein there isn't enough oxygen to support a proper ecosystem. We need to avoid excessive fertilizers, even with our high-octane annuals.

One solution to the above problem is to use slow-release pellets. We've found these very helpful at the greenhouse and sprinkle them in all of our hanging baskets. The tiny pellets contain the same inorganic fertilizer that you would normally mix with water, but it is trapped in a coating that slowly breaks down over a number of months so that the plants absorb all the nutrients in the fertilizer. Although this method doesn't deliver the "espresso shot" that the quick-release fertilizers do, it's lower maintenance and better for the environment.

Organic fertilizers are generally considered more environmentally friendly. They are also often comprised of very unglamorous materials, such as slurry, worm castings, bat guano and manure. There is a massive selection of them, and it would take much more space than I have to describe them all—nor have I tried them all. Be wary of organic fertilizers that don't tell you what's in them. For a fertilizer to be federally approved it must list its active ingredient. If it doesn't, you may be buying snake oil.

I am usually very hesitant to recommend a particular fertilizer and will only do so after it has proven itself to me year after year. The only organic fertilizer that has done this for me is actually not technically a fertilizer at all, but a growth supplement called MYKE. MYKE is short for mycorrhizae, which is a naturally occurring fungus. The fungus attaches itself to the roots of plants and forms a symbiotic relationship with the root system: the fungus gets a home and nutrients, and in return, its long strands increase the surface area of the roots.

Root systems are like human brains; the more surface area they have, the more powerful they are. When the mycorrhizae fungus increases the surface area of the roots, the roots become more efficient in capturing the moisture and nutrients available to them, which decreases waste and run-off and increases drought

MYKE has to be in direct contact with roots in order to work. Sprinkle some into the hole before you plant.

tolerance and overall health. A larger root system leads to a larger, more robust plant with larger, more numerous flowers.

The product MYKE is simply the mycorrhizae fungus in a dormant state. You apply it by sprinkling it in the planting hole so it's in direct contact with the root system. It has to be applied at the time of planting or it won't find the roots. MYKE isn't as fast acting as an inorganic fertilizer, and it takes about six weeks before you start to see the effects, but it will result in a much healthier plant overall. The only thing to remember about MYKE is that high concentrations of phosphorus will burn the fungus. After applying MYKE, don't use an inorganic fertilizer with a middle number higher than 20 (20-20-20 is fine). After a while you can probably get away with a middle number of 30, but don't use 10-52-10 at all. At Salisbury we've been using and recommending MYKE for the last few years and have been consistently impressed by its effects.

Each design and each plant will get one of three symbols to tell you how much fertilizer it needs to perform at its best.

⎺⎺⎽⎽⎟ This one means that the plants are light feeders and require very little fertilizer. I would add MYKE to the planting hole and then sprinkle some slow-release pellets on the soil. These plants are the easiest to fertilize but also tend to be the slowest growing. If they're hardy, one or two doses of 20-20-20 will be sufficient to keep them healthy for the year.

 This one means that the plants need an average amount of fertilizer. I recommend adding MYKE to the planting hole, along with a generous sprinkle of slow-release pellets on the soil. In addition, feed the plants monthly with a full dose of 20-20-20. If they start to look pale, increase the feeding to every two weeks.

This one means that the plants are heavy feeders and require lots of fertilizer. This category includes many of the most popular annuals. Add MYKE to the planting hole, and add a sprinkle slow-release pellets on the soil. These plants will also need a feeding of 20-20-20 once or twice a week. During their peak growing times in summer (at least

a month after planting), you may want to switch to 15-30-15 to keep them blooming and beautiful. Even though they are heavy feeders, don't mix your fertilizer stronger than it indicates on the package or you're throwing money away and could damage your plants. Rich green leaves and robust stems mean that the plants are getting enough food.

With high-performance annuals, ample fertilizer will keep the foliage a deep green and the flowers bountiful and colourful.

Don't always assume that more fertilizer is better. Some plants, like this stunning moth orchid, will get burned by too much fertilizer.

Question 5: Compatibility

When I was a teenager I inherited a second-hand, 30-gallon fish tank. I was giddy because I'd always wanted a soothing tropical fish tank, and hurried to the pet store to spend all my money. Thinking that a fish is a fish is a fish, I pretty much bought a wide assortment of whatever caught my eye, including a lot of neon tetras and a band of barbs. I went to sleep that night excited that I finally had a fish tank to call my own, so you can imagine the horror when I woke up the next morning to find the tank full of shredded tetra bits and some very pleased barbs. The barbs, an aggressive fish, had made short work of the passive tetras.

Sweet potato vine is normally a bully, but it is no match for the much more aggressive oxalis.

I realized that I violated the cardinal rule of fish tanks: don't put nasty fish in a closed space with nice fish. When you're creating a container garden, think of your container as a fish tank. It's an enclosed space where different species, with different evolutionary backgrounds, battle each other for sunlight and precious little water and nutrients. Within every beautiful summer container there's a merciless life or death struggle being waged.

The most beautiful containers pulse with tension because the competitors are so crammed in that each one is trying desperately to get a leaf over the other's leaf. Before you buy your container stuffers, find out a little bit about which plants go with which. A lot of people have spent a lot of money and time on containers that look great for only a few weeks until the dominant plant gobbles up the others.

Each plant in this book will have one of three symbols to tell you how aggressive it's going to be. You don't have to only put plants with the same symbol in each container. Think of the symbols as the fish store salesman who I wish had said to me, "I think I should tell you what will happen if you put those together." If you mix plants with different compatibilities, you will just need to be a little vigilant of protecting the passive plants (which is easy to do because, almost always, the more aggressive the plant, the easier it is to cut it back). That being said, sometimes it's fun just to put a lot of plants in a container and watch them battle it out. The symbols are fish based in memory of my poor little tetras who never had a chance.

 Goldfish are passive plants that grow slowly or sometimes barely at all. They include many of the most unorthodox container ingredients in this book, such as succulents. Often they're plants that are traditionally found inside and are sometimes more expensive than other plants; they tend to be the plants that you'd want to keep year after year. Aggressive annuals will gobble them up quickly and gleefully, so it's important that you protect them. If you plant goldfish with sharks, keep the clippers handy so you can rescue the goldfish!

Trout are middle-of-the-road aggressive. They will fight for their share of space but aren't out for world domination. In an unsupervised fight against a shark they will lose, just as they will eventually begin muscling a goldfish out of their way.

Sharks cover many of the most popular and fast-growing container stuffers introduced in the last 10 years. These plants are just plain imperialistic and will grow quickly in an attempt to control as much space as possible. Often they are the showiest braggarts available.

Types of Containers

Container gardening has become so dominant in gardening over the past decade that it's impossible for a book on design not to spend some time talking about the different styles and materials available. It's easy to spend all your time planning the details of how your flowers are going to look without giving any thought to the container you will use, but the container is a part of the container garden design. Its colour, texture and form play as much a role in the finished masterpiece as the plants do.

Every year, the containers in trendy styles and colours get snapped up

The type of container you use says a lot about how you want people to see your design. Without the urn, this design would have had a much different, less elegant feel to it.

quickly. Savvy gardeners always show up at my garden centre in April, when the big pottery orders arrive but before most of the plants are ready, so that they get the best selection.

The first thing I recommend with containers is to come to the garden centre with a budget in mind. The costs of containers range from practically free to astronomical. Also, the type of container that will work best in a garden will vary with region. For example, terracotta containers tend to dry out quickly, so they will work better in more humid regions, like southern Ontario.

Terracotta

The first pots ever used for container gardening were probably made of a fired clay similar to what we still use today. Terracotta is very popular around the world; when I tour through Europe, and especially Britain, I am adrift in a sea of terracotta pottery. It's cheap, versatile, easy to find, and in most of Canada it doesn't work well at all. Terracotta is a porous material that allows more oxygen to get to the roots, making for an all-around healthier plant—but only in the right climate. In our Canadian summers the clay heats up too much if it's in direct sunlight, and the roots dry out much faster than they would in a non-porous container. I see more terracotta in humid regions of Canada, but even there it can't be left out over winter because moisture

gets inside the porous clay, causing the pot to crack when it freezes.

Terracotta is still the best material, as far as pots go, to paint. For gardeners who love to decorate their pots as part of a whimsical garden, terracotta can be ideal. It is also ideal for herbs and for shade designs, as long as the containers are brought inside over winter. If you are lucky, after a few years moss might take hold and start to spread across the clay. The ability to grow moss is the real magic of terracotta, but we Canadians see it far too rarely.

If you use terracotta, try to soak the pot overnight before you plant in it,

Terracotta brings a European look to containers but needs to be dragged into the garage for winter.

and consider misting it occasionally. Dry clay is very absorbent and will pull much-needed moisture from the soil and the roots.

Glazed Ceramic

Many of the containers sold in Canada are glazed clay. Glazed containers are popular in Canada because they avoid many of the pitfalls of terracotta but keep some of its advantages. They are heavy, so you don't typically have to worry about them becoming top-heavy and toppling over. They are still clay, but the glaze inhibits gas and moisture exchange, so while the roots don't get the benefit of more oxygen, they also don't dry out as fast. If you're after colour, glazed pots are ideal. In early spring a large garden centre will typically have a huge selection of colours to choose from.

There are different qualities to the clay and the glaze that play a big factor in how long the pot will last. Of the two countries that export the most ceramics to Canada, the higher quality (though pricier) ones tend to come from Vietnam while the lower quality pots are usually made in China. The best quality glaze comes from Europe, with the best of the best being the slick German glazed pots such as Sheurich or SK.

If you're going to leave your glazed clay pots outside (and most people do since it's a huge pain to drag them in), they will need to be winterized.

Glazed ceramic pots are a popular look that can be left outside over winter if they are dry.

Make sure the pot is completely dry (if water gets into tiny cracks in the glaze, the pot will easily crack when it freezes), and I recommend covering the pot, especially if you're in an area with frequent freeze/thaw cycles.

Synthetic

This category covers everything from basic plastic "grower" pots to high-end fibreglass and resin. Until recently, the synthetic pots available in Canada tended to be low-quality, grower-grade plastics that often cheapened the look of a beautiful garden. Now, so many types and styles of synthetic pots are available that a gardener can create a scene that looks like it incorporates ceramic, terracotta, stone and metal.

Garden centres usually carry a good selection of synthetic pots, whether plastic, fibreglass or resin. If you're budget minded, or if you're looking for an inexpensive container to set

Synthetic containers are becoming very popular. They are more expensive but much easier to move around than ceramic.

inside a more expensive one to protect it, there are always lots of cheap plastic pots around. If you're in a European mood, the Dutch company Elho has an impressive range of plastics, though you might have to call around to find them. If you want a trendier, more stylish look, go with a large resin container; they are more expensive, but many people say they are well worth it.

There aren't many disadvantages to synthetics except that they can be so lightweight that you may need to put sand in the bottom of larger pots so they don't blow over in a stiff wind. The advantages are that they are fairly frost resistant, don't absorb water from the soil and often look convincingly like the stone or clay that they mimic for a fraction of the cost. They are also easy to clean.

Wood

If you want your garden to look as natural and as rich as possible, there's no better material to use than wood. Wood is my favourite material. Its harmonious, subtle tones are the perfect accent to any container garden. The advantages to wood, apart from its beauty, are that it doesn't pull water from the soil, it's remarkably frost resistant, it's fairly lightweight and it is a natural insulator that will help protect the roots from extreme temperature variations.

Because wood is a natural material, to prolong its life you will need to take some steps to protect it. Many types of softwood will rot easily—some in as little time as a year if planted into and left untreated. Cedar, having evolved in rainy coastal forests, is naturally resistant to rotting and is a great wood to choose. Consider lining your wooden container with plastic to protect it from the constant moisture of the soil. If you treat the container with a sealant, or if you use pressure-treated lumber, do not grow edible plants in it. Also, if your container is on the ground, consider elevating it with rocks or bricks to create air movement underneath and keep the bottom from rotting out.

Wooden containers can sometimes be hard to find, but probably the best

Wooden containers, like this half barrel, are easy and affordable to make if you're handy.

thing about them is how easy they are to make. There's no better winter project than to make the containers that you'll use in the garden come spring. Designs are easily available on the internet, or you can just experiment; the great thing about making containers is that if the ends don't line up exactly, it's not a mistake—it's drainage!

Soils and Potting Mixes

Soil may not be the sexiest thing about container gardening, but it is possibly the most important. The medium you use controls the amount of water your plants get, how easily their roots spread out, and how many nutrients they get; in other words, how beautiful your garden will be depends on the soil. The number of soils and soil additives available can be daunting, so I'll break it down a bit.

Soil-based Mixes

Soil-based mixes are the most common type of medium, the most readily available, and usually the cheapest, ranging from bags of black dirt to trendy potting mixes with flashy labels and catchy additives like water-absorbing crystals. Soil-based mixes tend to contain more nutrients than their soil-less cousins, resulting in slightly less fertilizing. They also hold water well, resulting in less watering; however, most roots need to dry at least a little between waterings so that they don't get waterlogged and succumb to root rot, which is a common condition in soil-based mixes. If the leaves of your plants start turning yellow, that's often them telling you that the soil is too wet.

Never use black dirt (also called loam) alone in a container, as it compacts around the roots when it's watered, collapsing air pockets and turning to mud. Air pockets are necessary so that the roots can dry out. Happily, there are many things you can add to black dirt to increase its porosity and allow water to flow through it more easily. Vermiculite and perlite, both inorganic and inert additives, act like Styrofoam in the soil to create air pockets. You can also add soil-less mixes to "cut" the dirt, as they are generally quite porous.

Keep in mind that soil-based mixes get very heavy when watered, so they may not be a good idea in hanging baskets, window boxes or large containers that you plan to move around. Because they retain so much water, you should make sure to use them only in the top foot or so or your container. Below that, where roots typically won't venture to in a season, it will stay wet and never dry out.

Soil-less Mixes

Although it may sound like an oxymoron, I've found that soil-less mixes consistently grow better plants than soil-based mixes. Soil-less mixes don't contain any black dirt. They are typically mixes of a number of organic and inorganic ingredients, with peat moss being the key ingredient in most Canadian blends. Many large commercial growers use soil-less mixes exclusively.

The main advantage of soil-less mediums is that they are very porous,

Soil-based mediums, like this potting mix, can clump if they aren't mixed with a lightening additive such as peat moss or vermiculite.

with long fibres that create ample air pockets for roots to dry quickly after watering. Delicate fibrous roots can also spread quickly through the pockets (about 80 percent of long-fibred peat is air), allowing the plant to absorb more moisture and nutrients.

The main disadvantage of soil-less mixes is that more porosity requires more watering. A plant that dries out quickly is not only usually very healthy but also very demanding; thus you will find yourself watering it more often. Also, peat moss shrinks like a dry sponge when it dries out completely, so if left too long it sometimes needs to be soaked a few times before the fibres open enough to capture water again. Some companies have come up with water-retention crystals or gels to add to the mix, with some success. Another disadvantage is that soil-less mixes have fewer naturally occurring nutrients than soil-based mixes do, so they require more fertilizing.

There is controversy over the use of peat moss in soil-less mixes. Peat is like coral; it's made of the accumulated remains of an organism, which in this case is sphagnum moss. Sphagnum moss bogs are considered non-renewable because they build up over centuries. In many parts of the world, using peat moss in gardening is environmentally verboten, especially in England where peat bogs are in short supply because many of them

Pure peat moss from a bog harvesting site at Premier in Quebec.

Sphagnum moss is a plant. When it dies it turns into peat and accumulates to form deep bogs.

have already been stripped clean for fuel, and conserving the bogs that are left is a major priority.

I toured a peat bog at the Premier (makers of Pro-Mix) operation in Quebec recently because I wanted to see the process for myself. I saw the original bogs, the fields where the peat was harvested, and the work that the company was doing to restore the bogs they had farmed. I realized that there is no need to feel guilty about using peat moss as long as it is from a company that has standards for sustainable environmental practices both in harvesting and reclamation. Canada has many more peat bogs than Europe does, but that doesn't mean they should be used irresponsibly. I recommend checking the environmental practices of a company before you buy their peat moss.

There are many available alternatives to peat moss, though none have become nearly as ubiquitous or as cost effective. Coir is a derivative of coconut shells and boasts the same excellent water retention. Numerous other products claim to be as reliable a growing medium, and many live up to that claim, so it's worth trying them if you are uncomfortable with using peat moss but would still prefer a soil-less medium.

Soil Additives

There are many soil additives that add or replace depleted nutrients in exhausted soils. Steer and sheep manure, soil booster and a variety of other products are excellent for bringing new life to dusty soils before you plant into them again. In container gardening, if the container was full and beautiful during summer, the

A peat bog being harvested. Ask your garden centre or the company you buy potting mix from if their supplier reclaims their harvested bogs.

roots will have bound the soil together into a tight ball by fall, so most of it has to be replaced anyway. At the beginning of the season, especially if you are using a soil-less mix, mixing in 25 percent or so of manure will both increase water retention and put much-needed nutrients into the medium, thus helping decrease your need to use copious amounts of inorganic fertilizer. For flower beds and raised gardens, spreading 2 to 5 centimetres of manure on top and mixing it spade deep will give the soil a spring nutrient perk.

One product in particular that is generating a lot of buzz is called Sea Soil. It's a relatively new product made on Vancouver Island and consists of a nutrient rich, composted blend of fish waste and the residue of industrial logging (the bark and organic bits left over from the sorting process). When I first heard the name a few years ago I thought that it was soil taken from the sea floor; I was happy to find out I was wrong and that its production seems to be completely environmentally sustainable. In only a few years it has amassed a huge following of gardening admirers. Although it's meant to be a top dressing, much like manure, some of our customers fill their whole gardens with it. It's very rich in a myriad of micro- and macronutrients, doesn't smell like fish and is completely organic. I recommend blending it into your soil-less mix before you plant so you don't have to use as much inorganic fertilizer during the season.

Choosing Healthy Plants

You can't have a healthy garden with unhealthy plants. Just as savvy grocery shoppers know to buy bread at one store and meat at another, many gardeners hop from one garden centre to the other during the few, frantic sunny weekends in May, gathering their various favourites along the way. Spotting the perfect plant is as much an art form as choosing the perfect cantaloupe, and like the cantaloupe, there are tell-tale signs as to whether or not the plant you choose will thrive in your garden.

When choosing your plants, the first thing to decide is where to go first. In

A healthy plant, like this 'Diamond Frost' euphorbia, should be well-branched and have firm stems.

the spring gardening world there are independent garden centres and there are box stores. The artificial choice that many gardeners believe they must make is between quality (garden centres) and low prices (box stores). This is often but not always true. Gardeners who are at a box store the day the truck arrives with fresh plants often find perfect quality, and many independents, including my own, are learning how not to be afraid of deep discounts and are challenging the boxes at their own game.

There are also things that independents offer that, though they are slowly improving, the boxes haven't been able to match: staff expertise, selection, and the proper environment for keeping plants healthy. I'm admittedly biased here; I'm the third generation of family owners of a greenhouse where our chief source of pride, and reputation, is the plants we grow.

The way I look at it, there are many things in life that are a chore to buy; plants shouldn't be one of them. Shopping for your plants sets the tone for the whole gardening season. In some ways it is the most important part of the season; it's where you meet the plants that will share your yard with you, the plants you'll nurture and grow to brag and perform for you. When our customers come through the door in spring, it's always with wide eyes and a head full of ideas and possibilities.

Buying gas is a chore, so it makes sense that you buy your gas at the cheapest place—period. Gardening is about discovery, creativity and fulfillment. To me, it makes sense that you buy your plants at a place where those things matter. It also helps to have confidence that the plants you're buying and are going to invest your time and energy into are healthy, and to be able to talk to people who know about what would look good with what and what will do well where.

Whether choosing a plant at an independent garden centre or a box store, you should know that the health of a plant is more than skin (or in this case flower) deep. It's common for first-time gardeners to choose the plant with the most wide open flowers, only to be disappointed when it's finished blooming. Look at the overall shape of a plant. Make sure your plant is full-bodied and not too leggy. Don't fall for the old in-full-bloom-but-no-leaves trick. Open flowers are good; healthy buds are better; a full, lush plant with healthy leaves and a strong stem is best.

Don't be shy about checking the roots by tipping the pot over (supporting the plant, of course) and tapping the bottom. It can damage a plant to just yank it out by the stem. You're typically looking for a well-colonized rootball with a nice balance of thick (tuberous) and fibrous roots. If chunks of soil fall away, the pot is too large, and if you have trouble removing the plant from the pot, it's root-bound. Usually the roots should be white, though the colour can vary with the species.

If the leaves appear pale and/or the main stem is weak and floppy, either the plant is not getting enough fertilizer or it was grown in too warm a place (which growers will sometimes do to put out a quick crop). Check for weeds; any weeds in the pot could spread to your container or flower bed. If the plant is strong, well-branched, and its roots are healthy, then any open blooms are a bonus.

Once you've bought your healthy plants, make sure they get a good start. If you like to get your plants early (because some of the most talked-about annuals do sell out quickly), it's important that they get some time outside even if they aren't planted yet. I suggest keeping them in a wheelbarrow so it's easy to push them outside if it's going to be a warm day and pull them inside if it's going to freeze. Outdoor plants need the sunshine and the elements of the outdoors; otherwise they will go downhill quickly.

Planting Tips

With your containers full of potting mix and your plants beside you, it's time to make some magic! Here are some good planting habits.

In one growing season roots won't grow very deep, and many of the most popular annuals have shallow root systems to begin with. When you're planting for one season, you need just 25 to 30 centimetres of good soil or potting mix. If you have a deeper container or bed, you're throwing your money away filling it with soil that roots are never going to reach. Fill it instead with a material that drains well, such as rocks or bark chips.

Moisten the soil in your container before you plant to reduce stress on the plant roots.

Pour the potting mix in and level it, but don't compress it with your hands or you will collapse all the air pockets that roots need to grow and breathe. Watering after planting the container will settle the soil naturally. Leave about an inch of space from the top of the potting mix to the rim of the container to allow for water to collect before it seeps in. This space is especially important for soil-less mediums that need to be watered often.

With the plants still in the pots you brought them home in, arrange them

Set the pots of your plants in the container in the design you want before planting to make sure your designs turn out like you planned.

into their design in the container. Now is the time to eye up your creation and make any last minute changes before you commit to it.

Don't pull the plants out by the stems; it damages them. Tip the pot over with your hand cupping the surface of the soil, and squeeze the pot gently until the rootball comes out. If the plant is root-bound, knead the rootball until it loosens up and you see fibrous roots sticking out of it.

Try planting the larger plants first, working your way down in size. Not only are smaller plants easier to fit in at the end, but working your way down in size will also give you a chance to see how the shape of the design is evolving as you go.

When all the plants are tucked in, gently work your fingers between them to make sure the soil is level all around. Water until there is a steady stream out the bottom drainage holes. Make sure

the stream of water you use isn't too rough on the new plants; they've been stressed enough for one day.

Finally, keep one tag from each plant handy so that, at the end of the season, you know exactly what worked and what didn't for next year.

The Pot-Drop

When creating gorgeous living compositions, we must often be innovative in order to turn our imagination into reality. Gardening is about your personal sense of creativity and wonder. When you look at a plant as a potential ingredient in a design, don't let your imagination be constrained by thinking that the way it has always been used in the past is the way that it must be used in the future. It's unorthodox to bring houseplants outside into a patio container, but I've always believed that gardeners make the rules and gardeners can always break them.

Pot-drop passive plants into aggressive containers to protect their roots and so you can safely remove them in fall.

Blending houseplants into containers full of annuals does have its hazards, however. They are often passive goldfish (see page 21) and don't do well in the survival-of-the-fittest environment of a container. And they are often fairly expensive because they are sold as plants that are meant to be kept for years on end.

When you're bringing inside plants outside, I recommend "pot-dropping" them into the container instead of transplanting them from one pot to another. To pot-drop, simply dig a hole in the container that is the size of your plant's indoor pot, plunk it in and backfill to hide the pot. This method of planting protects the plant's (often delicate) roots from any aggressive annuals it is sharing the container with and makes it easy to bring it indoors when the season is over. In fall, dig up the pot, wash it off, wash the plant with some safe soap to get rid of any pests, and you can bring it inside until next spring.

In addition to making it easier to plant goldfish with sharks, pot-dropping allows you to have plants with different moisture requirements in the same container because you have two enclosed spaces. For example, you could pot-drop a large succulent, which likes life on the dry side, into a container with bacopa and alocasia, which need more moisture. You can also use this technique if you want to put plants such as orchids, which need a different medium than most other plants, in a mixed container, or if you're using plants that bloom only for a short time, such as gerbera daisies, and then need to be replaced.

Planning Your Designs

In my books, I'm always promoting the joy of experimenting in your garden. It's easy to get caught in familiar habits year after year, but gardening shouldn't be the chore of filling the yard with plants every spring; it should be the delight of giving your yard fresh life after a long winter. The garden should be a place where you can go to relax and play and be nurtured by the life around you. There should always be something new to discover, combinations of plants that you've never tried before blooming amidst the old favourites. When you're planning your designs this year, try to make at least one container or bed completely new, using plants that you're discovering for the first time.

Before you can enjoy your new container or flower bed, you will need to have an idea of what will go into it. While doing something for the first time always requires a little more effort than repeating the same thing again and again, the planning stage is many gardeners' favourite part of the process. A lot of people start thinking about their gardens while they are still buried in snow. They look longingly out the window on a cold

February morning, dreaming about the summer bounty ahead of them.

How people plan their spring designs is a very personal thing. Like poetry or painting, planning is a creative process and people do it in their own way. Here are three methods of how to design for three different comfort levels.

Method 1: Using Recipes

Gardeners who are just starting out, possibly in their first suburban yard or apartment balcony, or those who would like more guidance, often use pre-published recipes such as the ones in this book. Pre-published recipes are great for people who need some confidence or who aren't feeling creative enough to be able to fill their basket with just the right kinds of plants to get a jump start.

Recipes take the guessing out of the planning process, but be mindful of where you are getting them from. The Canadian climate is much different than the climate in the southeastern U.S., California or even southern England, which is where many of the combinations in container gardening books are tested and published. Always check where your book was published, and if it was published in a climate that is very different from yours, proceed with caution. One of the reasons that I wrote this book was that I felt that Canadian gardeners needed recipes that would work for them, instead of having to always

You can make your garden seem a lot larger just by being aware of how you use the space in it.

rely on American recipes. Although some of the recipes in the book are from the American company Proven Winners, the ones I included from them will all work well in our colder nights and shorter seasons.

Remember that many books of container recipes are written by professional gardeners who have access to whatever plants they want to use. Sometimes authors don't think about how fiendishly difficult it might be for readers to acquire a certain rare hosta or a specimen-sized black mondo grass. Good recipes should use ingredients that walk the fine line between being relatively easy to find and yet exciting enough to bring a sense of adventure with them. It's a good idea to call around if you have your heart set on something, but never be afraid to substitute.

Method 2: Making Your Own Recipes

Once you have some confidence in which plants will grow well together, try making your own recipes. First, draw the outline of your container. Then, using your knowledge of plants or looking at a book of ingredients (again, it would be best to use a Canadian book), measure the diameter of your container and plan for an average of one plant per 7.5 centimetres of diameter (so a pot 30 centimetres across would have four plants). If you want your container to be full

and beautiful faster, try one plant per 5 centimetres of diameter, or if you are on a budget and are willing to wait longer, try one plant per 10 centimetres. These guidelines are only meant to be a starting point; the number of plants you use will vary with the types of plants and your personal taste.

Once your designs are complete, with your drawing in hand you can head to the garden centre to collect the ingredients you've decided on.

Method 3: Improvising

This is where the real fun can begin. I often suggest this method for gardeners who feel confident in how plants will blend together, both in growing and in design, though there's something to be said for jumping in way over your head and just having fun putting containers together. With improvising, the creative work happens at the garden centre, but I still recommend coming with an idea of the basic colours and/or textures that you want to showcase this season. My wife chooses a colour each year to build all the containers in the yard around, and every year it looks fabulous.

When you're in the garden centre, the number of options available to you can be quite daunting. I see it all the time: gardeners who come in (especially younger gardeners) just stop and stare for a moment at the number of plants that are available. At this point, if all you have in mind is to put a container together, you may not know where to begin.

Here's a tip that my wife gave me: the first step to putting a great container or design together is to find one element that inspires you. Instead of trying to look for the whole thing at once, look for one plant that inspires you and stands out from all the others. This plant will become your theme element, the one that will set the

Flower beds don't have to be full of flowers! Here, the deliberate bold red of the geraniums and bird bath jump out at the viewer and add some spice to the grasses bed.

tone of your design and around which you'll build your design. Discovering this plant is often the most exciting part of the process, and usually the thing about the plant that you fall in love with will become the central thematic feature of the design (whether the colour, the texture, the shape or a blend of these). For example, if you're most struck by the vertical architecture of a cordyline, your design will no doubt reflect that fascination.

The thematic element is often the largest element in the design (the thriller),

This innovative vertical petunia planter changes the context of the entire patio.

but it doesn't have to be. It could easily be a trailing vine that catches your eye or a flowering plant that will become the filler. To find it, browse up and down the garden centre aisles with an open mind and an eager eye. It's like looking for the perfect picnic spot or skipping stone at the lake—it will find you as much as you will find it. It will be the plant that catches and holds your eye, the one that you don't just glance over but keep looking at. Once you've found it, you've found the essence of your design.

With your thematic element on your cart, the garden centre will suddenly feel a lot less overwhelming. From this point on, let that plant be your guide as you build your design around it. Keep walking the aisles, seeing how the colours, textures and shapes of other plants will blend with it, and decide whether you want to create contrasts or harmonies in your design.

Other Planning Considerations

Context

Context plays a big role in the impact a container has. A 1 metre by 1 metre container will look massive next to a grouping of tiny herb pots, but in the midst of a grouping of 2 metre by 2 metre containers it will suddenly look very small. Before you head to the garden centre to buy your plants, take a walk through the areas where you're going to be showcasing your containers and flower beds to get an idea of the context of the space you're going to be planning for.

Angle of Perception

With three-dimensional objects, the appearance changes as we move around it and look at it from different angles. A container garden will look different if we look straight down on it than if we look at it from the side. The ideal angle of perception for a container (the angle from which it looks best) often determines where in the yard we display the container. For example, a basket with plants trailing over the side is best elevated or hanging, whereas an upright container is usually best on the ground.

Laying Out Your Yard

If you look back throughout human history, you'll quickly notice that the number three occurs again and again in almost every imaginable context. There is a certain magic about the number three. In designing, the number three is instantly dynamic, creating a sense of precariousness and tension wherever it occurs. Whether you are planning the container layout in your yard or the number of plants to put in the containers, try to think in threes (and if that fails, fives or sevens). A triangle is much more versatile from a design perspective than a square and much more interesting to look at than a line.

This park in Quebec is an ideal example of an excellent and careful layout, with annuals in the front and larger plants behind.

EVERY WORK OF visual art is made up of the elements and principles of design. Think of them as the genetics of art; they are the building blocks that make art what it is. I'm going to introduce you to the elements and principles of design that are most useful in container gardening. These aren't new concepts. As the fundamental building blocks of what we find visually appealing, you already use them in your garden designs. My goal is to help you to use them more deliberately. The more familiar you are with the effect that they have on the eye, the more creatively you can use them in your own living works of art.

The elements of design are the basic building blocks of art. There are about seven or eight of them, but some of them, such as line, aren't as applicable to container gardening as others.

The elements that are directly relatable to you as a gardener are colour, texture, and form and shape. All three will consistently come up throughout the book.

Colour is arguably the most important element of design in container gardening. I'll discuss the effects that individual colours and various colour mixes have on the eye.

Texture is the perhaps most underappreciated, yet most potent, element of design in gardening. How a plant feels (or equally important, how we think it feels) plays a huge role in how we see the container.

Form refers to the overall look of any three-dimensional object. In container gardening, the form is what the container looks like when all the ingredients are planted together. In gardening, unlike sculpture, the form

Every gardener uses the elements and principles of design, even if he/she doesn't realize it.

changes as the plants grow and compete, making form a very dynamic and exciting element. **Shape** refers to the shape of the plants making up the design. Form is the forest; shape is the trees.

If the elements of design are the building blocks of visual art, the principles of design are the rules that govern the elements. In other words, the principles of design are what make the elements of design effective. The principles include harmony and contrast, balance, repetition, scale and proportion, and movement.

Harmony and **contrast** are probably the most important principles to learn. They don't apply just to colour; great container gardens use harmony and contrast deliberately in colour, texture and form. Like yin and yang, the tension they create when they're balanced together can make a composition irresistible to look at.

We can use **balance**, or a deliberate lack of balance, to create either a sense of visual harmony or a sense of tension. In container gardening, balance is usually defined by how we arrange the different sizes of plants in the container and then how we arrange the different containers in a grouping.

Repetition of identical or similar elements in certain ways can have a big impact on how the viewer perceives the garden space.

In container gardening, **scale** usually has to do with the size of the plants as compared to their setting (i.e., in relation to the container or where it is displayed). Scale impacts how we see a container garden by giving it the illusion of looking larger or smaller than it actually is. **Proportion** deals with how large the plants are compared to one another. If one plant is a metre high and the rest are trailing plants, then the design's proportions are wildly different than if the plants are all the same size. The role of the focal point, or thriller plant, often determines what its proportion should be to the other plants.

Movement is a very exciting principle to me. We normally don't associate movement with gardens, but with several designs in this book I will show you how you can bring a dynamic sense of movement to your garden.

The principles of design are universal and show up in gardens world wide, like this stunning tropical pond garden at Kew Gardens in London, England.

The Elements
Colour

Colour is the most important element of design in container gardening. It can be combined in an endless variety of ways, and for many container garden designers, creating a vibrant blast of perfectly blended colours is the ideal goal. Blending colours is an art form, but you can start by learning

Colours and how they blend together are at the very heart of gardening.

the language of colour and getting to know the personality of each colour and how those colours behave when they're together.

Colours have so much personality and are so changeable in their moods that sometimes they seem almost human. A bouquet of purple flowers that is full of carefree exuberance at midday might become brooding and solemn at twilight; the difference between these two moods is in the amount of light. Colours are expressions of light defined by the colour spectrum that Sir Isaac Newton first described in the late 1600s after dividing a ray of sunlight with a glass prism. As gardeners we always have light in the back of our minds (e.g., the amount of light certain plants need). Artists are always thinking about light, too, and how different light waves interact with each other.

Many of us are afraid of colour, and who could blame us? The modern world is often colourless; it's normal to go through the day in a blur of off-white and beige. Our gardens are often the best place we can go to experience raw colour, and escape into the myriad of ways that it stimulates our senses. When you're planning the designs in your garden, embrace colour!

Choosing a Colour Scheme

Many gardeners use colour in many different ways; it all comes down to personal taste. Some gardeners bombard the eyes with strong doses of bright, pure colours such as yellows and purples, with each mass of flowers trying to show off more than the other. Other gardeners choose to be more subtle in how they use colour, blending and matching carefully for a more nuanced and contemporary palette. Your garden is your sanctuary, so you should fill it with colours that you love and in combinations that appeal most to you.

When it comes to mixing and working with colour, matching shades can be complicated, especially with colours that you aren't familiar with. Look at the colours in your wardrobe and/or your interior decorating scheme for inspiration. Gardening is a lot like fashion, after all, and the colours of your clothes will typically be the colours that most appeal to you. Also, because you see them all the time, you will have a better idea of how they interact and get along with other colours. This knowledge will give you a head-start in matching them in the garden.

Hue and Value

Every colour is a blend of hue and value. A colour's hue is its pure state (the colour on the colour wheel). The value of a colour is its lightness and darkness, which changes the hue into countless shades. While primary red is the hue of red, the countless variations that it can assume given different light conditions are its different values.

Value is a good thing to keep in mind when you're deciding what kind of light your container will be in (the exposure level that the plants need should be the most important deciding factor). Some flowers ignite in the noon sun with a brilliant radiance, and others get moody and melancholy in the twilight shadows. White and silver flowers are sometimes called "daylight extenders" because they tend to glow after dusk after absorbing sunlight all day.

Best design for daylight extending: Ascension, p. 110.

If you have colours that have the same hue but a different value (e.g., a light red flower and a dark red flower), the value contrast will make them seem far apart; one will appear farther away than the other. If the colours have a similar value (e.g., two red flowers that are from the same plant), the colours will seem close to each other; they will appear as being the same distance from the viewer even if they aren't.

Reading the Colour Wheel

There are three primary colours—red, yellow and blue—from which all other colours (over 15 million at last count) can be mixed and created. They are equidistant from each other on the colour wheel; you can draw a perfect triangle between the three of them. These colours are the elemental building blocks of the colour universe, and the eye recognizes them as such. Flowers that are a pure primary colour are always one of the first things we see in a garden. Hidden deep within the wavelengths of a pure red dahlia, a bright yellow pansy or a rich blue lobelia are the secrets to unlocking every colour you've ever seen.

The secondary colours—orange, green and purple—are derived from mixing equal parts of two primary colours (yellow and blue mix to create green, for example). As with the primaries, you can draw a perfect triangle between the secondaries on the wheel.

From these six colours we can keep mixing until we've unlocked every colour. Every colour on the spectrum is connected. They are qualities of light, resonating on the same spectrum even as they sometimes clash against each other.

The colour wheel is to a gardener what the periodic table is to a chemist: essential.

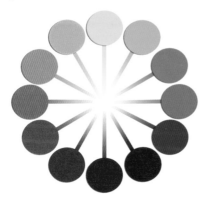

Analogous and Complementary Colours

Think of colours as people, arranged on a wheel according to their personality. Individuals who are beside each other on the wheel have very similar personalities and will get along well, while individuals who are far apart from each other have very different personalities and, if they are left in the same room together, sparks could fly. Being familiar with these basic rules about how colours do or don't get along is vital to taking your living art to the next step.

This 'Red Shield' hibiscus creates an analogous scheme with the deep red bromeliad to impressive effect.

If you want your container to have a harmonious colour scheme that expresses a sense of relaxation and unity, then choose colours that are analogous to each other. Analogous colours are all on one side of the colour wheel. The colours harmonize with each other because they reflect about the same amount of light back to the eye, so there is very little tension between them. When you are planning an analogous design, it's a good idea to make sure that one of the colours is a very pure, preferably primary colour. That hue will act as an anchor for the other analogous colours.

These red million bells create a complementary scheme with their own foliage.

Best design for an analogous colour scheme: Bellini, p. 178.

If you're looking for a design that will catch people's eyes and raise a few eyebrows, then you'll probably be interested in a complementary colour scheme. Complementary colours are opposite each other on the colour wheel. They each reflect a completely different amount of light back to the eye, so when you look at them beside each other, the eye and the brain are excited by the different levels of light coming in. These colours create contrast and tension in the design, which make it stimulating to look at, but be careful not to overdo the complementary schemes. With contrasting colours it's often easy to have too much of a good thing.

Best design for a complementary colour scheme: Prairie Breezes, p. 142.

An analogous colour scheme is any group of colours that are next to each other on the wheel.

A complementary colour scheme is any group of colours that are opposites on the wheel.

Triads

Triad colour schemes aren't used nearly as well in container gardening as complementary or analogous schemes are, but once you learn what they are I'm guessing you'll want to use them a lot in your garden. They have a simple construction. If you take your colour wheel and point to three equidistant spots on it (you should be able to draw an equilateral triangle between them), you will have a triad colour scheme.

Triads are perfect for designers who love the life and vibrancy of colour but don't want to create a high-contrast diva in the garden. Triads allow you to create designs full of colour but lacking direct contrast.

In the gardening world, triads are most often comprised of the three pure, primary colours. Creating a triad with the three secondary colours is a challenge because, in gardening, green can be neutral or active depending on how it's used.

Best design for a triad colour scheme: Eruption in Moss, p. 118.

A triad colour scheme is any three colours that are equidistant on the colour wheel.

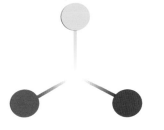

Monochromatic Colour Schemes

A monochromatic design takes analogous one step further and focuses the entire design on one central colour. Monochromatic designs are a deep exploration of colour and allow the designer to flesh out the nuances and hidden qualities of the chosen colour. If you really want to discover the varying moods and qualities that a colour has to offer, I recommend making a monochromatic design of it.

Because this colour scheme is so harmonious, it can risk becoming a bit boring. When you make one, try to create a sense of contrast in the textures and the shapes you use. Luckily, there are so many varieties of plants available for every colour that it's not difficult to find diversity within the same colour.

If you are adventurous, try creating several monochromatic containers, each a different colour, to form a grouping. For example, a triad of monochromatic containers would give each colour a powerful punch. It would also play with the sense of scale; a triad of monochromatic containers tends to look like one large container.

Best design for a monochromatic colour scheme: Pink Explosion, p. 182.

Warm Colours

Warm colours are rich, deep, invigorating colours such as red, bronze and

Red and orange are warm, inviting colours that seem to approach your eye as you look at them.

pink, colours that catch the sun and glow as if they could heat up a living room in winter. They seem to come close to you when you look at them, as if they are walking to you or you are being drawn in to them. This illusion makes them seem very intimate and personal. Warm-coloured flowers are often full of memories because they invite us to let our guard down and trust them.

Warm colours and the sun seem to thrive in each other's company, and the plants that boast these colours are usually, though not always, sun lovers. Plants such as red canna lilies, lantanas and dahlias seize the eye and demand attention with their intense colour. A design with several harmonious, hot colours planted together can be stunning; however, in a small space, all that invigorating, inviting colour may feel a little like painting a bedroom red.

Warm containers, and especially downright hot ones, will draw the eye to them naturally and get the blood flowing, so they can be placed farther away—in a part of the yard you go to explore and play rather than decompress. The tendency that warm colours have to appear as if they're moving toward you will also help to condense your garden space if they are far away, making the space seem a little more intimate.

Best design for a warm colour scheme: On the Boulevard, p. 114.

Cool Colours

On the other side of the palette are the cool colours such as silver, blue and green. Pastels are also cool; their soft tones will blend soothingly with each other as long as they aren't drowned out by red and orange. Cool colours seem to recede from us when we look at them. A garden full of cool designs can look serene and refreshing but can also seem as far away as the crisp blue sky.

Cool designs tend to have a more subtle interplay of colours than warm designs. Many contemporary designs use a harmonious cool colour scheme as a starting point. Cool-coloured plants also tend to boast more architectural appeal than their hotly coloured, braggart counterparts. What cool schemes lack in audacity they make up for in curiosity. Many of the newest and most provocative plants are best suited for cool designs; shimmering blue succulents and gleaming white datura would fit perfectly.

I usually recommend that people place cool containers close to their outdoor living space, where they can see the architecture of the plants up close, be refreshed by the colours and enjoy the daylight-extending properties that many of the plants have.

Best designs for cool colour schemes: Day at the Beach, p. 126; Parasol, p. 238.

The Cast of Colours

Shakespeare said the world was a stage and we all play our unique parts. The same holds true for colours in the garden. Each colour has its own dynamic, interesting personality. Colours are fascinating, both in how they interplay with others, whether through graceful harmony or invigorating contrast, and in how they look on their own. If you find a plant with a colour that you just can't take your eyes off of, don't be afraid to put it in its own container so you can stare at it as long as you want to without any other distractions.

The personality of colours is expressed in how they make us feel, reactions which are both universal and personal. I'm a sucker for the brightest possible yellow and the deepest possible burgundy (though not often together): yellow because it embodies a sense of pure joy to me and burgundy because it absorbs so much light that it's like looking into a tiny black hole. Deep, sometimes subconscious gut reactions will influence many of the decisions you make about colour. Listen to these reactions when you're choosing your plants. Of course, there's something wonderful about deliberately stepping outside of your comfort zone as well.

Cool colours such as white, silver and light blue can be crisp and invigorating to look at.

The universality of how colours make us feel has been tested and proved over millennia. All personal preferences aside, that yellow is happy and red is bold are rules you can depend on in every design you make.

Yellow

Yellow is my favourite colour, as I'm sure it is for many of you. It's the colour of light, of pure, honest joy that can't keep any secrets in its raw exuberance. When I was a kid, about the only thing I knew about painting was that I loved Van Gogh because he wasn't afraid of the colour yellow. Today when I look at his sunflowers or especially his Paris cafe, I feel a sense of inner satisfaction that few other works can give me.

In the garden, yellow contributes only beauty. Whether it's the symmetrical honesty of a sunflower or the warm glow of lantana, yellow only wants to catch as much sun as it possibly can and be beautiful. That's what makes

it so soothing to the soul even though it's a warm and exciting colour.

When I use yellow, I throw subtlety out the window and use the brightest, most joyous and satisfying yellows I can find—the yellow of Van Gogh's sunflowers or Wordsworth's host of daffodils. My favourite way to use it is in harmonious containers, where a vibrant, primary yellow centrepiece

Is there anything more cheerful than a big yellow sunflower on a sunny summer's day? I think not!

Yellow is one of the best colours for catching light. At midday, light yellow absolutely glows in the sun.

is highlighted by more muted yellow foliage such as lysimachia.

All that being said, I would still suggest using yellow sparingly. It is so invigorating and reflects so much light that a garden full of yellow would quickly become overwhelming. Think of bits of yellow in the garden as the magical kernels of spontaneous joy that pop up throughout your day, whether it's your favourite song on the radio or a surprise gift from a friend. The moments are made more special by their rarity, and the same goes with yellow. Every garden should have some, but ration it enough that you don't get tired of it.

Best design for use of yellow: Mediterranean Sunrise, p. 194.

Red

Red is the invigorating colour of boldness and passion. It's both intimate and alarming. To me, red is swirling dresses dancing the tango or the flag of revolution waving on the barricade in the musical *Les Miserables*. Throughout history, red has been heavily associated with blood. It's a potently symbolic colour and is one of the most common hues found on national flags. Red is also often used as a means of expressing a warning, such as with a stop sign or a fire truck. It grabs our attention as a colour of danger.

Red instantly draws our eyes to it. I bet the first thing you looked at in this picture was the red 'Lucifer' crocosmia.

Red bell peppers can light up a salad with their brash colour.

In the garden, red brings an instant sense of heat, sexiness and alertness. Red awakens the senses. It is arguably the warmest colour, and when you look at a pure, bright red flower, it seems to be moving toward you. In the sunlight, red can glow with such radiance that it almost feels like it could catch on fire, and it stirs the blood to look at it. When the day fades to twilight, however, and the shadows collect across the flowers, it suddenly becomes mysterious and menacing, as if hiding dark secrets.

I love red but suggest you use it sparingly. If you imagine a garden with nothing in it but shades of red, you can quickly see how its intense passion would quickly overwhelm the viewer. Use red when you want to make a container really stand out. If you mix it with analogous, warm colours such as yellows and oranges, it will be almost glow as a centrepiece. I don't recommend using much red near your outdoor sitting area because it is a colour that excites rather than relaxes.

Best designs for use of red: Canadian Afternoon, p. 146; Baby Elephant, p. 270.

Blue

I can't think about blue without thinking about mountains. In August 2009, I was with some friends on a gnarled and very active glacier flanking Mount Fay, which towers high above Moraine Lake in Banff. Above 10,000 feet the sky becomes a deep, rich blue that you could almost touch. As we were crossing the glacier, yawning crevasses opened up on either side of us, their icy walls tapering down into the ice and glimmering with a blue radiance so cold it was captivating. I'll never forget those two blues that day on the glacier; the rich, almost thick blue sky that went on forever, and the lifeless, mesmerizing blue tapering into icy depths.

Blue is a mysterious, complicated colour with many moods and layers. That afternoon, high above Moraine Lake, the sky filled me with inspiration and awe while the crevasses filled me with dread and dark fascination. The two blues were the same but different;

'Blue Waterfall' campanula produces scores of blue flowers in late spring.

they were both pure, both wondrous, but while the sky was an honest celebration of life, the crevasse was a shadowy and protracted mystery.

Blue can be just as varied in the garden. It can inspire carefree wonder and a feeling of freedom and expansiveness, or it can treat your eye to intoxicating depths as it lingers in shadows. Light blue is refreshing and calming to look at it, and darker shades have a delicious thickness to them. My eye tends to linger over dark blues as if it takes longer to take in the density of colour. No garden should be without some blue, as a tribute to the sky if for no other reason.

Robin's egg blue can express a playful, childlike innocence that will give your garden a sense of trust and adventure.

It's a cool colour, but it has a vast range from the icy, subtle interplay of blues on succulents to deep blue delphiniums. I recommend keeping some blue close to where you like to relax. Its ethereal sense of distance inspires quiet contemplation, which is perfect for unwinding after a long day. While warmer colours in the garden promote a sense of play, blue invites us to close our eyes and let ourselves drift away into a gorgeous big sky.

Best designs for use of blue: Small-Town Pickets, p. 154; Blue Bouquet, p. 202.

Purple

Purple is the traditional colour of royalty. For centuries, only the very rich could afford to buy garments dyed in expensive purple dye. It's a colour that evokes feelings of royal poise, sacrifice and powerful elegance. No garden should be without some purple, but how you use it is very much up to you. Depending on the value and context, purple can make a regal, elegant statement or it can infuse a childlike playfulness into the garden.

Purple is one of my favourite colours to use in the garden because it has so many moods that I can tap into as a designer. Dark purple is mysterious. It pulls the eye toward it, into the shadows that layer between purple petals or leaves. In container gardening, dark purple can range from proud and boastful to brooding and sinister, depending on what shapes and textures

'Devotion Purple' trachelium boasts vibrant purple flower heads in mid-summer.

you use. As it gets darker, it absorbs more and more light as it approaches ultraviolet and, eventually, passes out of our range of vision into a spectrum that only the bees can enjoy.

Light purple, which often crosses into lilac, is fun loving and inspires a light, playful mood. I recommend using it in areas of the garden where you want people to be encouraged to explore. It fits into many colour schemes, from analogous blends with other playful purples and light blues to complementary schemes with yellows, creams and pastels.

Best designs for use of purple:
The Crooked Grin, p. 186;
Tut's Treasure, p. 282.

Green

In 2004, I spent a month volunteering at a botanical reserve in the endangered Choco rainforest in northwestern Ecuador. It was so humid that I saw the sky once while I was there,

and the bills in my wallet had started to mildew when I left. I went into the jungle expecting to be overwhelmed by a rainbow of jungle colours. When I came out, it was with a new appreciation, bordering on wonderment, for the colour green.

In that rainforest I had been surrounded by green, more shades and

Dark green will bring a peaceful and secluded feel to a space.

hues than I would have ever thought possible. Everywhere I looked, whether at the detritus-covered ground, the bewilderingly dense understorey or the soaring canopy, the layers of green went on forever, budding, twining, growing, nourishing and breaking down. If the blues I saw on the mountain were the intoxicating wonder of a lifeless space, the greens in the jungle were life in overdrive.

We often take green for granted. It is the anchoring colour in the garden, and its potential is often dismissed as background noise like music in an elevator. But green is so much more than the colour of your lawn. Designs with nothing but greens can easily be some of most beautiful, albeit complex, in the garden. Plants such as gunneras, alocasias and musas (bananas), with their broad leaves transpiring so much that you can almost hear the process happening, can be the greatest show-stoppers of all. When you buy a plant, whether the flowers are going to be red, blue or yellow, you are buying the colour of its leaves as well.

Green isn't as passive in the garden as many people think. In containers with hot, bold red flowers, the green will balance the intense colour as if holding

Even though we're so used to seeing it, green can still be a very challenging colour to design with because it's the subtlest colour.

back a wild animal. Soft, emerald greens make us meditative and restful while dark, lush greens inspire thoughts of nurturing and growth. Every garden has green in it; the key is to remember that it plays as active a role as the other colours around it.

Green is the colour of new life and a fresh start. It is the colour we see most often, but also in many ways the most difficult to use in design because it is so nuanced and has so many faces. It is usually cool and has a refreshing impact, especially the bright greens of nasturtium petals and crisp lettuce. Lime green is very trendy right now because it's an invigorating, playful colour, and plants with lime green foliage, such as sweet potato vine and talinum, are flying off garden centre shelves.

Best designs for use of green: Striped Eruption, p. 98; Sherbet Waterfall, p. 274.

Orange

Orange is an oddity among colours because although it's a secondary colour, it doesn't carry a lot of sym-bolic or historical baggage with it, unlike its big brother red. It's a good colour to choose if you want the warmth of red without all the drama. The colour of Buddhism, it's a very intimate and comforting colour and is a perfect choice for designs near your outdoor sitting area. Unlike red, orange feels very safe and relaxing.

Orange is fairly rare in spring and summer designs, so much so that it often seems out of place early in the gardening season; fall is when it really starts to shine. When the trees start to glow with yellow and bronze, the orange colours in the garden seem to magically emerge.

The main drawback to using orange is that it can be hard to use in complex colour schemes. When it's paired with analogous colours it looks great, but

Orange is an uncommon colour in plants, which makes it especially eye-catching when it is used.

its complementary colour is blue, and they make a bit of an odd pair. It's also such an unabashedly warm colour that it tends to only work well in traditional designs, though I invite you to try to prove me wrong.

Best design for use of orange: Parade, p. 214.

Pink

Like orange, pink is closely tied to red on the colour wheel but escapes the drama that always surrounds red. It's a gentle colour, the colour of poise and femininity, but it can also be vivacious and full of life, usually as you add more to the mix.

Pink is a popular colour in container design thanks to the sense of innocence and optimism it brings. It's very versatile in its role. If you put it near your outdoor living space it will bring a sense of youthful cheer to the area, whereas

if it's farther away it will promote a sense of play and childlike wonder. It is one of the best colours for intriguing viewers, making them want to examine the garden closer to discover more hidden gems.

Pink is often seen in spring. When pink spring perennials bloom, it's a sure sign that winter has passed and the optimism of a new, green season can begin.

Best designs for use of pink: Pink Explosion, p. 182; Slow-Motion Explosion, p. 190.

White

Although not technically a colour, white is a powerful presence in the world of gardening and plays a significant role in the designs ahead. Its lack of pigment gives it its unique characteristic of reflecting every scrap of light that touches it. White

Pink expresses gentleness and femininity. Here, pink gypsophila blends with 'Artist' ageratum.

symbolizes purity and innocence in most western countries, but it symbolizes death in much of the east. Without getting too philosophical, white is often defined by a sense of absence rather than presence.

In the garden, white often isn't nearly as innocent as it first appears. In the midday sun it will glow with pure radiance but, depending on its texture, may collect dark shadows as twilight nears. Its ability to blend seamlessly into every colour scheme makes plants with white flowers, such as bacopa and lobelia, ideal fillers to add depth and body to your designs.

The best thing about white is that you can use it absolutely anywhere. It will fit as well around your indoor sitting area as it will splashed into the back of the garden.

Best designs for use of white: Ascension, p. 110; The Licorice Tower, p. 230.

Texture

As a boy, I would look at pictures of Van Gogh's "Starry Night" and Monet's "Water-lilies" and think they were pretty, but I didn't understand what the big deal was. As a man, travelling to Paris to see the masterworks in person, it was like I was seeing them for the first time. Staring at the way Van Gogh used texture, globbing and mashing and smearing the oil across the canvas (my nose probably closer

White lavatera is often overlooked for containers but grows into a shrub-sized mass of radiant white flowers.

to it than it should have been), I fell in love with the texture of the pieces. It was tantalizing, and I wanted to touch those stars and those water-lilies to experience that texture.

Gardening is all about touch. At Salisbury, I always see people touching plants, exploring their texture as if they are getting to know them before they decide whether or not to bring them into their yards. Texture is one of the most under-appreciated and important elements in garden design. While colour gets the spotlight and most of our attention, there is just as much "wow" factor and nearly as many options for texture as there are for colour. And, unlike the museum, there are no DO NOT TOUCH signs.

'Bunny Tails' fountain grass has a dense, fuzzy texture that is irresistible to touch.

To me, a stunning garden is a feast for as many senses as possible. Sight, of course, is the obvious one, but the more ambitious gardeners reach out to the other senses as well. You can create pockets of delicious smells using groupings of fragrant plants. Water features and plants with delicate foliage that catches the wind will fill the air with gentle sounds. Edible plants and herbs can bring taste into the garden, inviting grazing on sour cherries, stevia and nasturtiums as you wander through. And by experimenting with texture you can bring the sense of touch into your garden. Encouraging people to touch the plants engages them in a very active, very personal way.

We often think of texture as being a quality of very tactile plants such as a cactus or lamb's ear, but all plants have a sense of texture that our brain picks up on even if we're not consciously thinking about it. An alocasia, with its broad, glossy leaves, is very tactile, as are the sharp blades of a fountain grass or the dainty flowers of a diascia.

Texture is as visual as it is tactile. When you look at the soft fronds of a maidenhair fern or the stiff thorns of a golden barrel cactus, your mind tells you how it's going to feel even before you touch

Black aeonium has a texture as sleek and glossy as a viper, making it perfect for contemporary designs.

it. A variety of textures in the garden invigorates the tactile imagination and makes a garden come to life. While colour excites only the eyes, texture adds another dimension as you anticipate how it will feel as well as enjoy the way it looks.

Think of texture as the third dimension of the garden. Colour is the second dimension, the eye candy that no garden should be without. Texture is usually less showy but often more dynamic. When you're choosing the textures to put in your garden, remember that mixing textures is a lot like mixing colours: it's all about balance. While some containers might be harmoniously textured and some might be contrasting, keep in mind that too much of the former would bring so much unity to the scene that it would sanitize the sense of play, while too much of the latter would put you in danger of abandoning a sense of cohesion all together.

I'm always surprised by how many gardeners don't think about texture when they are planning their designs. Every plant has texture and every texture has a feel to it, so whether you are thinking about it or not, the texture of your garden is playing a big role in how your garden feels to everyone who visits it.

Best designs for use of texture: Dusty Country Road, p. 86; The Touchables, p. 102.

Form and Shape

In art, the overall form of the piece usually makes a bigger statement than the individual parts. Container gardens are no different; they are living compositions, and the first thing the eye notices when it looks at them is the overall shape of how the plants grow together.

It's easy to get swept up in the individual elements of your creation, but unless the plant is completely alone, garden design is all about the relationships between plants. A single plant in a container or a flower bed

The round shape of these calamondin oranges brings a sleek modern flavour to this container.

is like a line in a song or a fraction of a painted canvas; while it may be beautiful in itself, how it blends with the other elements is what will bring the whole composition alive.

Gardening is all about becoming infatuated with individual plants, which often makes it hard to remember to think about how your new favourite will blend with others while you're admiring it at the garden centre. The best way to make sure your finished creation has an attractive form is to hold different plants up beside each other while still shopping so you can see how their shapes, and

Rustic grasses, like this blue oat grass, bring a rugged and versatile sense of form to designs.

not just their colours, blend together. I often see savvy gardeners arranging plants on their carts while they are still in the garden centre.

One of the things that makes designing with plants so unique and challenging is that, unlike other three-dimensional sculpture, the form of a container garden will change and evolve throughout the season. If the plants in the container aren't compatible with each other, then one plant will become dominant over the others, which will change the balance of the composition. It can be very exciting to watch your work of art grow and change as the months roll by, especially when the form changes in ways you didn't expect. However, if you spent a lot of time and energy planning an exact and precise shape, you may be disappointed in a month or two, particularly if you planted aggressive shark plants with passive goldfish plants. Form can be hard to pin down sometimes.

Types of Form

Designs in the garden are often imitations of the patterns that exist within nature. This imitation means that container gardens usually have an organic sense of form, which means the design embraces a sense of a unified whole rather than celebrates the individual plants. Beautiful containers are often microcosms of the way plants grow naturally, only much more condensed and deliberate, of course. Several of the designs in this book take that sense of imitation to a whole new level and try to represent a specific scene in nature.

Best design for traditional form: Canopy, p. 78.

Best design for representative form: Coral Dreams, p. 266.

Contemporary container gardens often have very geometric forms that emphasize angles and lines over a unified organic harmony. Architectural plants such as succulents and rigid grasses such as cordyline fit perfectly into many modern designs. Contemporary containers tend to celebrate the shapes of different leaves and flowers and pay less attention to the overall form than more traditional, organic designs.

Best design for contemporary form: Kaleidoscope, p. 82.

The Principles
Harmony and Contrast

Think of harmony and contrast as the yin and yang of designing. They are the two most dominant principles of design in container gardening because they apply to colour, texture and form. Harmony and contrast are, in their basic sense, a measure of how relaxing or how stimulating your designs are. Harmonic designs, whether they have

'Lemon' osteospermum and sweet potato vine harmonize with each other and soothe the eye.

'Melon' osteospermum and sweet potato vine make a stark, modern contrast with each other.

analogous colour schemes, similar textures or a classically symmetrical sense of balance, are excellent for areas of the garden where you like to sit and unwind at the end of a stressful day. Contrast is ideal for containers or areas in the garden where you want to invite people to walk over and explore.

The human eye is automatically drawn to harmony because it presupposes a pattern and underlying order. When we look at contrast, it is to subconsciously try to make sense of it and find an order within the disorder. When faced with contrast, we seek harmony. When we find harmony, we find relief and start to relax.

When you're dealing with harmony and contrast, always keep the idea of balance in the back of your mind. Whether in colour, texture or form,

Use black when you want to create dramatic contrast, like this sweet potato vine and petunia.

too much of either can lead to a disappointing overall effect. A garden that is completely harmonic would be relaxing to the point of boring. Instead of being encouraged to explore and play, the visitor would probably be invited to take a nap. Conversely, an utterly contrasting garden would cause stimulus overload. Without a relaxing point of order to rest our eyes on, we don't know where to look and the experience can quickly become unnerving.

Think about what you use different areas of your garden for. If you have a spot that you like to go to unwind at the end of the day and just relax, try filling it with soothing, harmonious designs and colour schemes. If there is a spot in your garden where you like to explore and play, where you go to awaken dozy senses, then fill it with contrasts to make it invigorating. Once you know how to effectively use this principle, your designs will stop traffic every summer.

How to Create Contrast

Contrast is what makes your garden leap up and wow people; it is where you can really express a sense of your individuality in your designs. Contrast can create pockets of your garden where the senses love to linger, play and discover all there is to find, or it can make a container that makes jaws drop open and starts every conversation with, "How did you do that?"

Contrast is created by resisting a sense of pattern; it holds our attention as we try to make sense of it. A black sheep in the middle of a white herd not only draws our eye to it and holds it but also gives the rest of the herd a sense of scale and acts as a focal point. The black sheep doesn't take anything away from the visual interest of the white herd; on the contrary, it makes us appreciate aspects of the rest of the sheep (how many there are, the shape of the herd, etc.) that we might not have noticed without a contrasting point of reference.

Contrast doesn't always have to be white against black. You can create variety by using several degrees of contrast. If you try to use nothing but opposites, you'll tire your viewer out quickly, but if you use many degrees of contrast, with different elements contrasting each other in different ways, your garden will have a deep sense of play that comes from the layers of contrast you've planted into it.

Using Colour to Create Harmony and Contrast

A refreshing thing about using a design element as multi-faceted as colour is that there are rules we can rely on for what looks good and what doesn't. Every gardener should keep a colour wheel as a reference; a colour wheel is for gardeners what the periodic table is for chemists. Following the colour wheel, especially for new gardeners, can feel like using a cheat sheet in a test.

It's a universal rule that analogous schemes create a sense of harmony while complementary schemes create contrast. That rule isn't built on personal taste; it comes from the science of how the brain reacts to varying levels of light. For example, yellow reflects the most light on the wheel and purple absorbs the most light; they are the two most contrasting colours. As a designer, you know for a fact that if you put yellow and purple together you'll create a sense of tension; it's a refreshing guarantee in a hobby with so many variables.

Purple osteospermums and yellow marigolds create an eye-popping contrast that excites the eye.

Colours can be beautiful alone, but, just like humans, their true character comes out through their relationships. How close colours are on the colour wheel (i.e., in the colour spectrum) is what creates a sense of harmony and unity or contrast and chaos between them. The tension you see when opposite colours are beside each other is the clashing together of two different wavelengths of light. If the contrasting colours are placed close enough together, the contrast becomes so crisp that the colours can seem to vibrate against each other.

Harmonious designs are soothing to the eye. They capture a refreshing sense of unity in the way the colours naturally flow in and out of each other. Harmonious designs turn a garden into a ballet. They are great at the end of the day for relaxing jangled nerves along with a glass of wine while watching a long Canadian sunset. The yin of colour design, harmony is about gentle transitions and a soothing reconnection with colour.

Best designs for colour harmony: Streams of Gold, p. 294; Summer Elegance, p. 210.

Contrasting colours create the "wow" factor in the garden. They are a clash of opposing colours that catch the eye and stimulate the senses. Contrasting designs excite us, make us curious, and draw us into the opposing colours. Contrast is the yang of colour design, and it is what gives a garden the energy and exuberance to awaken our senses even as the harmonies soothe them.

Best designs for colour contrast: Parade, p. 214; Calypso, p. 222.

Using Shape to Create Harmony and Contrast

Form is the overall composition, but within that, the individual plants all

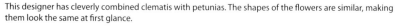

This designer has cleverly combined clematis with petunias. The shapes of the flowers are similar, making them look the same at first glance.

relate to each other via the principles of design. A myriad of shapes, whether they are leaves, flowers, stems or anything else within the composition, all play against each other to create the grand form. The shapes of the plants are what create the contrast and harmony that make the overall form dynamic.

The shapes that make up the overall form of your container determine how much harmony or contrast there is within it. If the shapes within the container are alike and harmonious, then the overall form will have a calming sense of unity that makes it pleasing to look at. But if the shapes are contrasting, then the container will have an extra layer of dynamism to help excite the eye.

Harmonious designs might have similarly shaped leaves or growing habits that bind the plants together into a pattern that the eye can grab onto. If you made a container of ferns, with their distinctive fronds, the form would be harmonious, though not very dynamic. Throw a black alocasia into the mix, and you are balancing harmony with contrast and a sense of playfulness. As with colour and texture, too much harmony of shapes will cause your creations to become so unified and pleasing to look at that they will stop being exciting to look at, whereas too much contrast in your shapes will have the eye craving a sense of pattern and unity.

Best design for harmony of shapes: Margarita, p. 122.

Best design for contrast of shapes: Jester, p. 262.

Balance

Nature is full of things that balance each other—often an intricate sense of balance can be found at the heart of many things in nature. In container gardening, the sense of balance we want to achieve as designers typically determines the overall shape that the design will take. Where you put the largest ingredient (the focal point, or thriller) typically determines how

In symmetrical balance, there are the same amount of fillers and spillers on both sides of the thriller.

balanced or unbalanced the container will be, as the other ingredients will naturally revolve around it.

Normally we think of balance as harmonious, but a savvy gardener can easily use imbalance to create a sense of visual tension. Whereas a container with a centred focal point is balanced and generally pleasing to the eye, putting your focal point off-centre creates a tension within the shape of the container that catches the eye. Gardeners seeking to create modern containers often choose to use a sense of imbalance to make them more visually striking.

It's good to remember that balance is mostly about how the eye moves across what it sees. If you have two very prominent or bright ingredients at either end of a large container, the eye will move between them, seeking the balance point.

Symmetrical Balance

Symmetrical balance is the simplest balance, wherein the shape is the same on either side of an imaginary, centred vertical axis (line). Symmetry creates a sense of unity and calm and is pleasing to the eye. Classic-looking containers are almost always balanced; in fact, some gardeners consider achieving a perfect sense of symmetry as the goal for the ideal container. Symmetrical balance is excellent for stand-alone containers that have the largest ingredient planted in the

centre and the other ingredients tiered down around it. It is most common to use analogous colour schemes to add to the sense of harmony.

If you want to make a grouping of containers look like one large container, then try to create a sense of symmetrical balance within the group. The symmetry will unify them and help to make them appear as one.

Best design for symmetrical balance: Lavender Skies, p. 218.

Asymmetrical Balance

Asymmetrical balance is achievd when the container is balanced but not centred. You can achieve a sense of pleasing balance with the focal point not being centreed, but it needs to be offset on the other side with a smaller element.

Asymmetrical balance is more stimulating to the eye but can be slightly more challenging to create than symmetrical balance.

Asymmetrical balance is most common in containers with a modern or architectural twist to them. They don't embrace the classic container orthodoxy of "thriller, filler, spiller" as much as symmetrically balanced designs do. The more unbalanced you make it, the more tension you are creating in the outline.

Remember that with balance and imbalance, just as with harmony and contrast, it's important to find the middle ground. If you have too much balance, like too much colour harmony, you risk making your garden so relaxing that it becomes boring. If you have no balance and complete randomness throughout the garden, you may bring on a sense of disorder and chaos.

Best design for asymmetrical balance: Beneath the Surface, p. 278.

Using Colour to Create Balance

Our eye is drawn to bright, bold colour much more than to dull colours. If you want to achieve a sense of balance in a design, then you can easily add an ingredient with a pure hue flower, like a red dahlia, that will stand out more than the others. The primary hue will attract the eye, making that side of the design look larger.

Best design for using colour to create balance: Coral Dreams, p. 266.

Repetition

One of the easiest ways to create harmony and a soothing sense of unity in the garden is through repetition. Simply repeating the same or similar elements in two or more spaces will allow the eye to take everything in at once, using the repeating elements to

This Edmonton gardener uses repeating pots to frame the entrance to his beautiful show garden.

bind the garden together like strands of thread pulling fabric together. However, too much repetition will make your garden so unified that it could lose the sense of adventure that comes from a little bit of contrast and chaos thrown in.

Patio stairs are a great place to use repetition for visual impact. Placing small to medium-sized, simple containers (often one striking element will do) on each step will create a sense of dynamism by drawing attention to the different levels, which the eye loves, and will provide a stimulating introduction to the patio itself and the containers there. For stairs, I recommend that the

You can use repetition in flower beds, too. Small beds around trees are easy to make and have a big impact.

pots be all the same, as they will typically serve as accents to the larger containers on and around the patio.

Best design for use of repetition: Small-Town Pickets, p. 154.

Varied Repetition

The best way to reap the rewards of repetition (a pleasing sense of unity) while avoiding the potential pitfalls (too much unity can get boring and lose its playfulness) is to use varied repetition. You can do this by repeating some elements while changing others. For example, filling the yard with only pots of sunflowers would be visually stunning but wouldn't arouse curiosity; there would be so much "wow" factor that there wouldn't be any room left for a sense of play. However, if you use sunflowers strategically across the yard, in various contexts, they will bring a sense of unity while still keeping the flashes of unpredictability and whimsical playfulness that make a garden truly exciting.

Varied repetition works very well in simple groupings of pots. Just by taking three pots in different sizes (often they are matching colours and styles but don't have to be) and planting them so that they accent each other, you can easily create a visually striking container tableau in a vacant corner or dead space in the yard.

Best design for use of varied repetition: Margarita, p. 122.

Visual Groupings

The human brain loves to find patterns even where there are none. If you draw two dots of a blank piece of paper, the brain will draw an imaginary line between them. Draw three dots and it will pretend there's a triangle there. This tendency for us to visually group our world into patterns is called Gestalt psychology. Knowledge of Gestalt can be a powerful tool in the garden designer's artistic tool box.

In the garden you can use this self-organizing principle to play with the eye and create a sense of unity while still maintaining a sense of contrast and excitement. If you arrange three pots in a grouping and use yellow pansies in each one, the yellow will pull the pots together like a rope binding them in our minds. You can then use the rest of the space in the pots to play within that grouping as much as you wish, either by planting similar elements to create varied repetition or by planting completely different elements to create a sense of excitement. Whatever you do after

If you group several similarly themed containers together, they will appear from a distance like one impressive design.

Groups of containers are a great way to show off vibrant colours.

you plant those yellow pansies, the brain will turn the pots (as long as they are fairly close together) into a visual grouping, immediately condensing the space and making the visitor feel relaxed and comfortable.

You can use visual grouping across the whole garden just as easily as across a few pots. If you plant sunflowers across the garden (you can tell yellow is my favourite colour), being careful that the eye can always see a few at a time, the viewer's brain will bind them together, bringing an immediate sense of unity to the garden. As the gardener, and having created that unity, you can then play with contrasts and exciting elements within it knowing that the sunflowers are binding the garden together.

Best design for use of visual grouping: Devonian Postcards, p. 138.

Scale and Proportion

Container gardening is about a lot more than just making one design. When we look at a deck, patio or garden space our eyes don't jump from one container garden to the other. We see the scene as a whole, and our eyes balance every element of the garden against every other element. As a container garden designer, you should have an idea in your mind about the overall look you're trying to achieve. If you want a particular garden space to showcase cool colours and soft tones, then one container full of bright orange and red million bells would look out of place.

Our eyes compare the elements of a garden to each other in terms of size as well as colour and form. Scale refers to the size a design as compared to the other elements around it, whether that is other container gardens, a table or the house.

You can use scale in your garden to highlight the designs that you want to be the dominant statements in the space. If you make a grouping of containers, a practice that I recommend, you can highlight the central container by making it larger than the others. As you scale down the container, perhaps from five or six different plants in the central design to one plant in the simplest designs, plant them in progressively smaller containers to keep a harmonic sense of scale.

If you want to create a sense of scale that shakes things up a little, try grouping some very small, simple containers around a large, complicated central design. The contrast in the scale would be the first thing the eye registered when looking at it.

Best design for use of scale: Falling Angels, p. 302.

Focal Point

In painting, the focal point is the first place the eye goes to when looking at

When compared with the Victoria harbour, this line of baskets looks tiny.

a work and tends to be the organizing element around which the rest of the painting is ordered. In container gardening, the focal point is usually (but not always) the largest, most dominant plant, also known as a thriller. In most containers, the focal point is the central plant and defines the design's look and feel.

The focal point is often emphasized by all the other plants around it. If the largest element is in the centre and all the other elements build up to it, the centre will be emphasized because the other elements will have drawn our eyes to it. When the plants around the focal point build up to it, it's called radial design.

Often the focal point declares itself as such simply by being the biggest

This is the same basket in a street lamp outside the Empress Hotel, now looking much larger thanks to the different scale.

Focal points are often in the centre of containers with the other plants around them.

In a wide container, such as a window box, you may want several focal points side by side.

plant, but you can make a plant a focal point through clever use of design. Our eyes are excited by contrast. If you want an element to really stand out, separate it either through size—the focal point is usually the largest—or through texture, colour, shape or a combination.

As the designer, you can decide what you want the proportion of your focal point to be to the rest of the plants. If there's a big difference in size between the largest plant and the second largest, then it will bring a modern feel to the design. If you scale all the plants to flow subtly and organically from largest to smallest, then your container will look more traditional in flavour.

Best design for an organic focal point: Show-Off, p. 174.

Best design for a modern focal point: Parasol, p. 238.

Movement

While movement isn't something that many people would think applies to container gardening, it can be just as powerful and evocative a design principle in gardening as it is in sculpture or painting. In most visual arts, the artist uses tools such as angles, blurred lines and optical illusions to create a sense of motion. In gardening, we need only plant the right ingredients together and watch the magic.

Creating a sense of movement in the garden isn't all that hard. All you need are plants that reach upward into the sky with wide, branching stems and flowers. There are a lot of options out there, and I'll discuss them more in the feature designs throughout the book.

Best design for use of movement:
Taking Flight, p. 258.

'Pony Tail' stipa grass catches every breeze and is ideal for brining a sense of movement to the garden.

The Devonian

Height: to 1 m • **Spread:** to 50 cm

I LOVE FERNS BECAUSE they are some of the most direct links we have with the dinosaurs. Unchanging for hundreds of millions of years (I think we could learn something from that), ferns are familiar to everyone and are so versatile that creative designers will always find ways to reinvent them in new compositions. This container is my salute to ferns, and with them as my thematic element I began to browse the greenhouse looking for ways to explore their prehistoric theme.

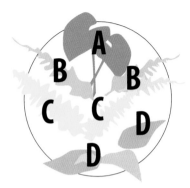

A Alocasia 'Jurassic Dark'

B Plumosa fern

C Boston fern 'Rita's Gold'

D Zebrina tradescantia

Recommended container size:
40–55 cm across

I like to tell a story with my containers in the hope that the viewer feels compelled to linger a little longer while looking. This design mimics a Devonian jungle, with a horizontal canopy layer arcing over a dense undergrowth of ferns.

Here, the golden ferns (I chose 'Rita's Gold' over traditional Bostons because it has a neater, more compact habit) and the tradescantia contrast below while the deliciously delicate fronds of plumosa fern and the thick leaves of a 'Jurassic Dark' alocasia provide textural interest in the "canopy." If you want to be a purist, you could try using only ferns; a large garden centre will have more than enough variety of textures, forms and even colours.

Protect this one from the sun and remember to keep it consistently moist. In humid regions you should be able to expose it to late morning sun. If brown scorch marks appear on the ferns, protect it more.

It won't need much more fertilizer than Myke and slow-release pellets when you plant it, but it will appreciate some generous showers from the hose nozzle to increase the humidity. It would be ideal beside a sheltered water feature.

Foxtail fern (*Asparagus densiflorus*) grows slowly into dense green clusters that are ideal for designing.

Ⓐ Alocasia 'Jurassic Dark'

Alocasia plumbea; elephant ear

Broad and looming, this one can also be hard to find but is worth the search. At Salisbury we had to have it shipped in from California. If you can't find it, just ask for a dark-leafed alocasia or colocasia.

Ⓑ Plumosa fern

Asparagus setaceus; emerald fern

This fern is often hard to find and takes a long time to grow, but its lacy foliage suspends itself in the air horizontally with a delicacy that is ideal for any Oriental-themed container.

Ⓒ Boston fern 'Rita's Gold'

Nephrolepis exaltata; golden Boston fern

With a compact, more manageable growth habit than the classic Boston, golden ferns are better for container gardening, with the lime-green one being adaptable to modern designs. Make sure the roots stay moist, but still provide good drainage, and take it easy on the fertilizer.

Ⓓ Zebrina tradescantia

see p. 200

A (above); B (below)

Designing with Ferns

There are so many kinds of ferns that it would take a whole book to list them all! Most of the ferns available in garden centres have been hybridized to be fairly easy to take care of. Two of my favourites are the leatherleaf fern (photo A), with its strikingly prehistoric foliage, and the maidenhair fern, which is at the other end of the texture spectrum with lacy, delicate fronds and a graceful habit (photo B).

C (above); D (below)

Ferns can make a big statement as well as other, flashier annuals can. Asparagus fern is an old favourite that adds a billowing sense of drama to this otherwise simple design (photo C). Be careful of using asparagus ferns in the home over a carpet, though; they tend to drop their share of needles.

Ferns are one of the best accent plants because their foliage is so unique (photo D). The horizontal sweep of a plumosa fern puts the finishing touches on a foliage container, its dainty fronds contrasting with the bulkier foliage around it.

Canopy

Height: to 1.2 m · **Spread:** to 80 cm

WHEN I SAW this container sitting on an Earl's patio, it instantly reminded me of the jungle. With its lush flora and intensely competitive look, it is a splash of rainforest that will make the whole yard feel a little fresher. In true jungle fashion, textures and colours contrast frantically with each other while the masses of tropical leaves grow into each other so that it's impossible to tell where one ends and the other begins. If you love thick, dense foliage bursting out of its container, this recipe won't disappoint!

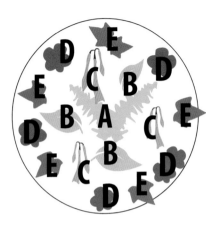

A Australian tree fern

B Iresine 'Blazin Lime'

C Fuchsia 'Gartenmeister Bonstedt'

D Impatiens 'Accent Mystic Mix'

E English ivy

Recommended container size:
50–70 cm across

There is a method to the madness; the plants are layered in a classic "thriller, filler, spiller" style, but they are just so lush that the layers have grown into a single mass of leaves and colour, and delightful chaos seems to have ensued. You can either protect certain plants from each other or, like the law of the jungle says, let the strong survive.

The centrepiece is the exotic and dramatic Australian tree fern, which is like a portable rainforest for any design. It can be hard to find, however, so call around and be patient. If you can't find one, a large garden centre may be able to order one in for you. Once you get your hands on it, keep it in the house through winter (make sure to mist it daily so the fronds don't dry out).

If you have a flair for the dramatic and have a large, semi-sheltered sitting area, try grouping this container with some smaller pots using simpler mixes of the same plants. Everyone who visits will start a conversation about it.

Iresine can bring a lush tropical splash and will thrive in partial shade as long as it's in a sheltered spot so it can stay warm through cool nights.

A Australian tree fern
Cyathea cooperi

Native to the steamy jungle of northern Australia, tree ferns have a look all their own. They are ideal for containers, with the stem taking up virtually no room at soil level, but they are even less drought tolerant than other ferns—make sure yours never dries out. They have a very delicate root system, so I definitely recommend keeping yours in a pot to protect it from the more aggressive iresine and fuchsia.

B Iresine 'Blazin Lime'
Iresine herbstii; beefsteak plant

Usually known to be red, the green variety, with its creamy veins and crisp red stems, provides much of the leafy mass of this container. Iresine loves heat and fertilizer, so although it needs shelter from the afternoon sun, a hot spot is ideal.

C Fuchsia 'Gartenmeister Bonstedt'
Fuchsia triphylla

'Gartenmeister' is an upright fuchsia that will never go out of style. Its lipstick red pendulums hang in clusters up and down the plant, contrasting sharply with the dark green leaves. It's the best annual for attracting hummingbirds, so you will have some animals in your jungle.

D Impatiens 'Accent Mystic Mix'
see p. 272

E English ivy
see p. 312

The Hummingbird Fuchsia

Because attracting butterflies and hummingbirds never goes out of style, the plants that attract them best will always be at the top of a savvy gardener's list. 'Gartenmeister' fuchsia has remained popular while many other, older fuchsias have

A (left)

B (above); C (below)

fallen out of fashion. It's arguably the best annual available for attracting gorgeous pollinators and is one of the more unique fuchsias around. A large, shrub-like habit makes it ideal as the centrepiece of a large container (photo A).

'Gartenmeister' has the built-in contrast of vibrant red flowers on dark green leaves, and it looks tropical enough to fit seamlessly into a jungle-themed container (after all, what's more jungle than wildlife?). There is a variegated variety available that has the same growth habit (photo B).

The tree fern, though still rare, is popping up more and more in containers (photo C). Its lush, tropical

fronds blend perfectly with other tropical annuals or foliage (I plan to try one as the centrepiece for an all-fern design). If you're looking for one, call the garden centres early (March or April) and ask if you can order it in.

Kaleidoscope

Height: to 1.2 m · **Spread:** to 1 m

I WISH YOU could see this design in person. It would be a perfect still-life for an aspiring artist. From every angle is a different kaleidoscopic layering of shape, colour and texture. It's a perfect example of how a living composition changes and shifts as it grows; every week you'll discover a new alignment of shapes and angles that wasn't there before!

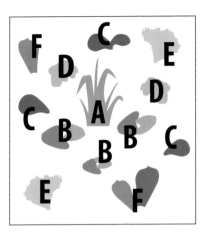

Ⓐ Cordyline 'Red Sensation'

Ⓑ Eucalyptus 'Silver Drop'

Ⓒ Kalanchoe

Ⓓ Sedum 'Autumn Joy'

Ⓔ Kale

Ⓕ Aeonium

Recommended container size:
  60–70 cm across

The dance of shapes is what makes this recipe spectacular. Without a flower in sight, it blends ingredients that are rarely used together, opening your mind to exciting new design ideas and potential combinations.

The Tasmanian-born eucalyptus arcs outward with layers of silver-blue discs so that it's in the foreground of almost every sightline. The other ingredients create a dense nest of unique forms, all competing against each other for your attention. It would make an attention-grabbing focal point in a yard with a contemporary flair.

Put this container in the hottest spot you can find and watch it thrive. Many of these plants are succulents, so let it dry slightly between waterings and don't over-fertilize it. If you want to keep a plant over winter (such as the cordyline), submerge its pot in the container you're using for your design so you don't have to disturb its roots in fall.

With its compact form and wavy texture, don't underestimate how valuable kale is in designing.

Ⓐ Cordyline 'Red Sensation'

Cordyline australis; Bauer's dracaena

No stranger to containers, here its stiff blades stand in stark contrast with the swirling discs of the eucalyptus. If you bring it inside in fall, make sure you wipe it clean of spider mites, especially if it has been a hot, dry summer.

Ⓑ Eucalyptus 'Silver Drop'

Eucalyptus gunnii

This plant takes the container from interesting to extraordinary. Although it has slightly finicky watering requirements (it needs to dry slightly between waterings or it may rot), once it gets established and starts to branch into the summer sun, there's no stopping it! At the end of the season, make sure to enjoy it as a cut flower.

Ⓒ Kalanchoe

Kalanchoe thyrsiflora; paddle plant

One of the most unusual container stuffers, paddle plant boasts broad paddles that tinge with red along the sides when the nights are cool. It's a succulent and likes to stay on the dry side.

Ⓓ Sedum 'Autumn Joy'

Sedum spectabile; stonecrop

This perennial starts the season with an interesting texture, then explodes mid-summer into broad flower heads that thrive well into fall. Not often seen in containers, you can either take it out and plant it in the garden in September or enjoy its warm colours in the container well into October.

Ⓔ Kale

Brassica oleracea; flowering cabbage

Ⓕ Aeonium

Aeonium spp.

Designing with Succulents

Succulents are enjoying a surge in popularity because of their incredible design potential, which gardeners everywhere are just beginning to explore. I love succulents because when they get together they are a feast of textures and shapes for the eye to explore and devour. We encountered so many amazing succulent containers in preparation for this book that choosing which ones to include and which ones not to was difficult.

Try to find a large succulent selection from which to choose from, and take your time. The colours of the foliage are more subdued than flower colours, so if you've never designed with them before, try to get to know them first. Their magic is in the subtle dance of hue and textures, but used right they create containers that I could stare at for hours (photo A).

Succulent planters don't need to be devoid of flowers. Echeverias provide soft-spoken pink spikes (photo C) while the common kalanchoe (available almost anywhere flowering plants are sold) pulses with intense, vivid colour (photo B). You could also pair succulents with portulaca or gazania for a burst of colour.

A (above)

B (above); C (below)

Dusty Country Road

Height: to 70 cm • **Spread:** to 70 cm

TEXTURE ISN'T JUST about how something feels when we touch it; it's also about how our minds tell us it's going to feel before we touch it. This container is almost irresistibly touchable, with so many textural goodies that it had my brain going five different directions about how it was going to feel. The colour scheme is a soothing, cool harmony of silvers and blues that relaxes the eye as the textural collage excites the imagination.

- Ⓐ Blue oat grass
- Ⓑ Fescue 'Elijah Blue'
- **Ⓒ** Echeveria
- Ⓓ Lamb's ear
- Ⓔ Artemisia
- Ⓕ Woolly thyme

Recommended container size:
45–65 cm across

This design is perfect for providing a focal point that draws people's attention (it will pull them toward it to investigate the textures) without being the loudest one at the party. If you want to add more atmosphere to it, try an old barn-board fencepost to enhance the rustic feel.

The plants in this container need an exposed, sunny spot. The container in the picture was against a south-facing brick wall. Water sparingly because many plants in here hate having their feet wet and prefer to dry between waterings.

A lot of these ingredients are perennials, so if you're planning to plant some of these kinds of perennials in a bed, try planting them in a container first to enjoy them as a focal point before putting them in the ground in fall. Get the best of both worlds— gorgeous container stuffers and then perennials to enjoy year after year.

Rustic designs that are full of texture often benefit from elaborate containers with a sense of age to them, like this cast iron urn.

Ⓐ Blue oat grass

Helictotrichon sempervirens

A rugged, very hardy perennial, blue oat grass has a perfect colour for this harmony, and its distinctive prairie-like heads add enough texture to help balance it vertically. Unlike some larger grasses, you won't have to trim it.

Ⓑ Fescue 'Elijah Blue'

see p. 156

Ⓒ Echeveria

Echeveria spp.; rosette succulent

Echeveria brings a crisp sense of architecture and form to the mix, providing the cleanest lines and keeping the container from becoming just a little too wild. Throughout the season expect the lower leaves to fall off as they grow up the stalk, like a palm tree.

Ⓓ Lamb's ear

Stachys byzantina

This is the one we all love to touch! Many of us have memories of discovering the delightfully furry "ears," and we'll be drawn to this recipe as soon as we realize that the lamb's ears are there just waiting to be rubbed.

Ⓔ Artemisia

see p. 240

Ⓕ Woolly thyme

Thymus pseudolanuginosus

Another touchable classic, thyme is an old-fashioned groundcover that's being rediscovered for its design potential in containers. Its texture and colour give it a lot of versatility, and its instantly recognizable shape makes everyone take a second look, often to say, "Is that thyme in there?"

Rustic Designing

The feature ("Dusty Country Road") feels as if John Wayne could be leaning on a fence next to it smoking a Marlboro. With the right ingredients it's easy to create a cool-themed container that uses bold textures to create a wild, rugged, Western feel. Choose some ingredients with an informal, even messy growth habit (thyme, artemisia, etc.), and contrast them with architectural plants with formal lines (echeveria, oat grass, eucalyptus, etc). Add some rocks and an appropriately rustic container for the finishing touches.

A splash of colour, as long as it's not overwhelming, will add some zest to your silver, Western-themed container without distracting from its cool, slightly macho feel (photo A).

Adding some trailers and grasses will allow the eye to wander vertically, and the messy lines contrasting with the formal lines will hold interest (photo B).

If you're intrigued by this style, I encourage you to use these guidelines to create your own rugged design. Even with few flowers, a well-designed container will keep the eye exploring through the maze of line and texture. This style would fit especially well in a garden that uses a lot of cool colours (photo C).

A (above)

B (above); C (below)

Hot Potato

Height: to 1.5 m • **Spread:** to 70 cm

A RECIPE DOESN'T always have to include an inventive mix of completely different ingredients. Often several varieties of one ingredient create a striking sense of harmony. At the greenhouse we plant up hundreds of big hanging baskets each spring with nothing but blended colours of sweet potato vine, and savvy gardeners eagerly snatch them up, knowing that they work either as accents or as a focal point. Sometimes the most novel way to use a plant is the simplest one.

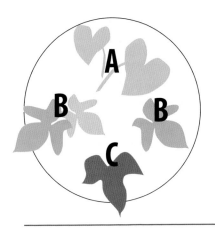

A Sweet potato vine 'Sweet Caroline Light Green'

B Sweet potato vine 'Sweet Caroline Bronze'

C Sweet potato vine 'Sweet Caroline Purple'

Recommended container size:
25–35 cm across

This container would make a better accent than a focal point. Just as sweet potato vine is at its best when it's accenting colourful, fuller plants in a recipe, this container would be at its best in a grouping with other containers of flowering annuals. That being said, it can be striking used on its own (like in the photo below), but you would have to really, really like it if you want to frame your sitting area with it.

Give sweet potato vine healthy doses of fertilizer and water, then stand back and watch as it grows massive in the summer sun. Make sure to put it in either a tall container or, preferably, a hanging basket, where its long, curving vines can hang far below and wave in the breeze.

The downside of growing sweet potato vine is that it's not very drought tolerant, so make sure it's in a large enough container that you don't have to water it constantly in a heat wave. Wait until night temperatures are above 4° Celsius before you put it outside; it's very tender.

Blend 'Illusion' Series sweet potato vine with other thin-leafed annuals and grasses for a container with delicate, serrated shapes.

A Sweet potato vine 'Sweet Caroline' Series
Ipomoea batatas

There are several different series of sweet potato vine, and most of them perform exceptionally well. The big differences are in leaf shape and colour. My personal favourite is 'Sweet Caroline' because I find the colour to be richer than the others, with an almost three dimensional quality.

Single Ingredient Designs

A (above)

While this book has a lot of complicated designs in it, complexity doesn't always equal creativity. Your designs should be an expression of yourself; simple designs can be stirring and confidently elegant. The feature ("Hot Potato") is a blend of several colours of the same plant. If there's a plant you particularly love, try planting it on its own in a carefully selected pot. You'll probably be surprised at how much it can impress you when it has you all to itself.

Sometimes the simplest designs can make the boldest impression. Meg and I found a calamondin orange tree that was striking on its own in an overly tall, rustic pot (photo A). With nothing else to distract from it, my eye explored its sleek curves and gentle green leaves at leisure. I never thought a fairly common houseplant could look as impressively contemporary as it did there.

My mother, Val MacMillan, has a small, decorative wheelbarrow that she fills with kale (photo B). Kale is

B (above); C (below)

one of those plants that becomes more fascinating the longer you look at it. While the eye might glance over it in a mixed container, on its own you can focus on its exquisite textures, intricately curled leaves and surprisingly clean symmetry.

In Quebec City we came upon a container of 'Tuscan Blue' rosemary planted on its own in a park (photo C). While I'm used to seeing rosemary planted in herb gardens and even in mixed containers, I hadn't appreciated how gorgeous a plant it really is. Its branches reached out in all directions like a Bonsai tree, at once lush and sparse, gentle and rugged.

Herbs, Herbs, Herbs

Size: depends on design

CREATING INNOVATIVE compositions in containers and flower beds isn't about spending a lot of money on the newest, trendiest annuals on the market. It's about looking at plants with fresh eyes and using them to their full potential. This entry isn't about one specific design; it's here to encourage you to think about herbs in a different way. You'll be amazed at how gorgeous those humble herbs on your windowsill can be when given the chance to shine in fresh, gorgeous designs.

Recommended container size:
depends on design

Herbs are plants for all senses: they are striking to look at, comforting to smell, interesting to touch and, of course, a refreshing treat to taste. They need not be confined to a clay pot or your vegetable bed. In an ornamental design they draw visitors closer, instantly inviting them to smell, touch and taste and thus begin to explore the garden more intimately than they would just with their eyes.

The beauty of herbs isn't in big, bragging flowers. Like succulents, herbs are more subtle in their beauty, treating the eye to an array of glossy and course textures, vibrant greens and dusky purples, and a vast array of smells and tastes.

The best part about herbs is that they grow thicker and fuller the more you pinch off the tasty new growth. When my wife and I barbecue or make a salad, a pizza or even certain cocktails, we go into the yard and tear off some shoots to use. Take care that you don't use any pesticides or herbicides around the herbs, and make sure they're not in contact with poisonous plants.

All herbs are sun lovers, and most of them (with rare exceptions, such as watercress) like to dry slightly between waterings. The only herb

I typically don't recommend for mixed plantings is basil because it needs to dry more than most and doesn't like playing nice with others.

The sky is the limit for how creative you can be with herbs! Many of them can adapt to almost any container as long as they have light.

🅐 Dill and cilantro
Anethum graveolens and *Coriandrum sativum*

Stunning in large containers, these giants grow very tall and have strong aromas that become even stronger when you touch them.

🅑 Parsley and mint
Petroselinum spp. and *Mentha spicata*

A triple-curled parsley with heads as broad as your palm is stunning in a mixed planting, and flat-leafed parsley is becoming more and more popular. There is a bafflingly large selection of mints available, from Moroccan to banana to chocolate to English (make sure you plant English mint in a container where its roots can't reach the ground).

🅒 Sage and rosemary
Salvia officinalis and *Rosmarinus officinalis*

These classic Italian herbs love the hot sun and are surprisingly drought tolerant. Ask your local garden centre what varieties of these herbs they have; recent introductions have included 'Barbecue' rosemary and stylish purple sage. Rosemary is exceptional on its own if you have the right variety; I recommend 'Tuscan Blue,' although it does lose flavour after a few years once it becomes woody.

Designing with Herbs

The more you use herbs, the more you will come to love the colour green. In herbs, green is so vibrant and full of life that the colour becomes as delicious to the eyes as the plant is to the taste buds.

Herbs have such unlimited potential in the garden that it would take me a whole book just to begin to talk about how you can use them in your designs (let alone ways to eat them). Here are a few tips in the small space that I do have.

A (bottom left); B (above)

Last summer we mixed different types of basil (sweet and purple-leafed) with hot peppers and some lemon grass for a Thai cuisine–inspired container that would be a perfect touch for a themed dinner party (photo A).

Herbs and vegetables can have brilliant colour! Cherry tomatoes clustered on the vine (photo B) are just as vibrant as any flower. Peppers can boast some brilliant colour too, and bell peppers come in a host of different colours, from greens and reds to purples and rich browns.

Striped Eruption

Height: to 80 cm • **Spread:** to 70 cm

IN THIS BOOK I've focused mostly on outdoor compositions, but there are countless things that you can do with "houseplants" as well. This example is meant to get your creativity flowing. Not only could our homes use a lively indoor composition to break the monotony of our long winter, but they could also use some extra freshness during summer. Take a look at the houseplants you have lying around and ask yourself, "If I put these into a container together, how would they look?" You might be pleasantly surprised by the answer.

A Calathea

B Asparagus fern

C Liriope

Recommended container size:
30–40 cm across

There are so many different plants that you can use for indoor containers. Typically the choices you have available to you depend on how much light you have. If you have a sunroom or a very well lit area, you can get away with using some tropical annuals inside, such as New Guinea impatiens, sweet potato vine or coleus. Without adequate light, even tropical annuals will get leggy and pale indoors. However, you can always use ferns, orchids, leafy tropical plants or flowering indoor plants.

Designs with houseplants will give you a new appreciation for green. Green has the most varied mood, depth and shade of any colour on the wheel. Here, the most obvious design element at play is the contrasting textures between the broad, luxurious calathea leaves and the mischievous (and yes, a little messy) asparagus fern. A 'Magenta' dracaena in the centre would add even more rich colour to complement the calathea.

The plants in this design aren't hard to find (except the liriope, which I recommend replacing with a more interesting 'Magenta' dracaena anyway). Calathea and asparagus fern are readily available at large garden centres.

The fact that they are common ingredients only reinforces the fact that we often just don't look at houseplants as having the same design potential as we do annuals. We typically carry a stereotype in our head of houseplants as being boring and utilitarian, but if you open your mind to their potential, they will always surprise you.

Crotons (*Codiaeum variegatum*) are readily available houseplants that will bring vivid colour indoors as long as they have adequate light.

Ⓐ Calathea

Calathea spp.

There are many shapes and sizes of this staple foliage houseplant available, and it is easier to take care of than its flashier counterpart, alocasia. Make sure to keep the soil consistently moist, as is usually the case with houseplants because they are almost always tropical species. There are many varieties, but they are usually sold as an assortment.

Ⓑ Asparagus fern

Asparagus densiflorus; sprengeri fern

This fast-growing fern is inside/outside versatile. If you don't like the mess it makes (it tends to shed needles, especially if it dries out), then ask for foxtail fern, which is slower growing and requires misting but makes up for it by giving you elegant, rounded stems.

Ⓒ Liriope

Liriope muscari; lilyturf

Liriope is a popular ornamental groundcover in the United States but rarely finds its way to Canadian containers because it's fairly forgettable. It blooms dense spikes of small, violet-blue flowers and forms a loose tuft of long, thin leaves. I recommend using a different annual grass, such as 'King Tut' papyrus, or another houseplant, such as a 'Magenta' dracaena, instead.

Indoor Container Design

Indoor containers don't need to be grandiose, and if you look around your home you will probably find that you already have all the ingredients you need for a fresh new design sitting on coffee tables and tucked away in bathrooms. Combining houseplants can also bring new life to tired plants that have probably been largely forgotten about except for when watering time comes around. One thing you can do is blend a couple of small houseplants in a shallow pan or

A (bottom left); B (above)

dish. As long as the pot has drainage, they will grow in any container. Two or three small ingredients are enough to create a soft and original addition to a room (photo A).

If you want to use blooming plants year-round, simply leave a space the size of a standard plastic pot (I suggest 10–15 centimetres in diameter) in your planter. This way you can always keep a fresh blooming plant in the centre, like an orchid, while the foliage around it grows continually larger and more impressive (photo B).

The Touchables

Height: to 40 cm • **Spread:** to 40 cm

CONTAINER GARDENING is one of the most creative kinds of gardening there is, and like everything creative, the more you do it, the more excited you get about it! We had a container gardening contest with the Salisbury staff where everyone was invited to get involved. We had some amazing entries come in, and it wasn't easy choosing one to feature for this book. This container was designed and planted by Mario Salazar, our head grower and a wizard with all things green.

Ⓐ Lamb's ear

Ⓑ Curry

Ⓒ Chrysocephalum 'Flambe'

Ⓓ Licorice plant 'Limelight'

Ⓔ Lamium 'Beacon Silver'

Recommended container size:
35–45 cm across

I chose this container because it's such a delicious exploration of textures. Mario chose plants for how they feel, both to our fingers and to our brains. Remember that texture is as much mental as it is physical. Much of the delight we get from looking at an interesting texture is from the anticipation of how it really feels. The plants here are all textured, and combined with the cool colour scheme and symphony of contrasting shapes, this design would be an alluring treat in anyone's garden.

There's a sense of the wild here, a lack of centralized order that fits with the many textures and shapes. It's a container about exploration and play, which is often the most rewarding gardening you could ever do.

As one of the best growers around, Mario has naturally put ingredients together that have the same basic care needs. All of them are drought tolerant and thrive in full sun.

Nothing here is overly aggressive, so this container is maintenance free.

I would keep it close to you on a sunny deck or patio where you like to relax. Every once in a while you'll catch yourself running your palm across the lamb's ear or rubbing the curry between your fingers to capture its scent.

'Iron Cross' rex begonia has unique leaves that feel as if they've been stuccoed.

Ⓐ **Lamb's ear**

Stachys byzantina

This classic textured perennial boasts soft, furry leaves and a dusky silver colour. It blooms in mid-summer, but I'm not a big fan of its bloom. You can keep it year after year by transplanting it into the garden in fall.

Ⓑ **Curry**

Helichrysum italicum

This spiky-leaved herb has a potent aroma when it is rubbed and needs the same conditions as a rosemary plant: dry and sunny. You can also cook with it if you like.

Ⓒ **Chrysocephalum 'Flambe'**

Chrysocephalum apiculatum; Australian daisy

Much of the delightful chaos in this container is the work of this wonderful annual. With its sparse growing habit it tends to send stems everywhere, each one punctuated on the end by a crisp, yellow rosette.

Ⓓ **Licorice plant 'Limelight'**

Helichrysum petiolare

Licorice plant is a groundcover that is often used as a trailing container stuffer. It can double as a filler, and its textured, lime green, licorice-scented foliage has made it sought after for container design. It is drought tolerant and easy to take care of when established.

Ⓔ **Lamium 'Beacon Silver'**
see p. 252

Thinking About Texture

A good way to think about how we feel texture mentally before we feel it on our fingers is to think about a slug or something equally distasteful. Just looking at it makes you take a step back in disgust as you think about how slimy it is, even though you haven't physically touched it.

A (bottom left); B (above)

The same goes for things that we want to touch. We touch with our mind, then our hands. Savvy designers know this and sometimes add deliciously textured plants to pull the viewer closer to the design.

Many textured plants are perennials and fit well into designs with a cool palette. 'Silver Mound' artemisia is a delicately tufted perennial that invites you to take a step closer and is a great way to get people to investigate your container further (photo A).

Lamb's ear is one of the most beloved and well-known textured plants (photo B). Even if you're one of the rare few who haven't felt its soft, almost pelt-like leaves between your fingertips, you will get the idea of how it feels just by looking at it. Adding one of these is a sure-fire way to pull people closer to your design.

Foliage Fantasy

Height: to 1m • **Spread:** to 70 cm

I BELIEVE THAT gardening is a constant journey of discovery and rediscovery on so many levels. Every year, hundreds of new varieties of annuals hit garden centre and box store shelves, often driven by massive marketing dollars and all promising to be the next big thing. Before you run out to get the trendiest new plant, try to rediscover some that you haven't thought of in a while. This recipe is all about using rediscovered plants.

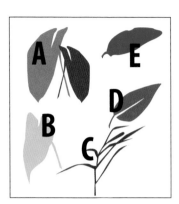

A Colocasia 'Black Magic'

B Arrowhead plant

C Pteris fern

D Chinese evergreen

E Peace lily

Recommended container size:
40–55 cm across

Making a design with only foliage is often a journey into a whole different way of looking at how plants blend together. Instead of measuring bloom colours against each other, you start to become aware of leaf colours, textures and subtle harmonies and contrasts that you might have missed had there been flowers everywhere.

Once I started designing with foliage I got hooked, both because I realized the beauty of the plants themselves and because the process taught me how to see more than flowers when I designed with colourful annuals.

None of the plants here are new. Most of them are houseplant staples that people have been using (and forgetting about) for decades. When they're blended together, however, they become a subtle collage of textured surfaces and richly coloured leaves that would be perfect to bring an oxygenating splash of the tropics to a sheltered patio or sitting area.

This container needs to protected from the afternoon sun (and even from the morning sun in dry regions). It's very low maintenance once planted because all the ingredients are fairly slow growing. It doesn't need much fertilizer but will need to be kept consistently moist.

'Polly' alocasia *(Alocasia amazonica)* is a starkly modern foliage annual that is perfect for contemporary containers.

Ⓐ Colocasia 'Black Magic'
Colocasia esculenta; elephant ear, taro

This old-fashioned water plant has started to hit its stride as a container stuffer. Its big leaves contrast with the softer coloured tropical plants and shade the container, bringing a slight sense of jungle canopy.

Ⓑ Arrowhead plant
Syngonium podophyllum; arrowhead vine

This old-fashioned houseplant demands very little care and gives a lot of reward. Misting it occasionally will keep its leaves full and healthy in indirect light or shade.

Ⓒ Pteris fern
Pteris spp.

Pteris fern is one of the most exotic-looking ferns you can get that is still easy to care for. It will appreciate a gentle misting now and then and shouldn't be allowed to dry out, but apart from that it's maintenance free.

Ⓓ Chinese evergreen
Aglaonema vittata

Although they are as old-fashioned as plants get, there are a surprising number of varieties of Chinese evergreens to choose from. They are really quite resilient and can handle a fair amount of neglect.

Ⓔ Peace lily
Spathiphyllum spp.

Foliage Containers

Foliage containers tend to have a big-leafed plant as a centrepiece. Big leaves make such a big splash that it's hard not to be tempted by them, even if you start your design thinking that you won't use them. They are more versatile than many people give them credit for. We found a container at Butchart Gardens in Victoria that used

A (bottom left); B (above)

big leaves with a white palette, which surprised me because they are normally associated with dark designs. The Tahitian bridal veil (*Gibasis geniculata*), an old-fashioned houseplant, clustered and spilling out the edges of the container, added a sense of tradition and nostalgia to an otherwise modern design (photo A).

At Salisbury we love experimenting with plants. We planted a big-leaf container using a massive 'Persian Palm' alocasia, a black colocasia and an ornamental banana plant. The result was a surprisingly easy container that collected a lot of admiring comments from people coming and going (photo B).

Ascension

Height: to 1 m • **Spread:** to 1 m

WHEN THIS BASKET catches the afternoon sun, it's absolutely radiant. Its vivid whiteness shone so much that we had to put it in the shade to take a picture that wasn't overexposed. It's a joy to have in the garden because of its crisp, bright purity, but don't be fooled into thinking it's simple; there are a lot of elements at play to produce that effect. Four levels of annuals create a subtle sense of ascension, with the flowers becoming more delicate as the eye moves upward.

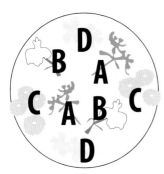

A Euphorbia 'Diamond Frost'

B Lobelia 'Laguna White'

C Petunia 'Supertunia White'

D Bacopa 'Snowstorm'

Recommended container size:
30–40 cm across

The basket relies on four varieties of white flowers, each with a different growth habit, to create its height. At the top, euphorbia is arching upward as if to merge with the clouds, making the top layer the most delicate with the smallest, most airy flowers. Below that, lobelia grows in tight bunches of dime-sized flowers and cascades out the sides, providing the bulk of the flowers that we see because it grows farther outward than the petunias and covers them a little. The petunias are the largest flowers and act as the anchor layer for the container, their feet planted firmly on the earth. At the bottom, the bacopa trails downward like roots and can seem to be the only thing keeping it all from floating away!

White is endlessly versatile and will look great anywhere, with any colour. If this much white isn't your thing, you can be creative with the colours while still keeping the levels that give this design so much body. Try lilac lobelia, or pink or blue petunias. As long as you stay within the types of annuals, you can switch up the colours freely.

This container loves to shine in full sun. Fertilize it often to keep it looking its best.

Linda Mundell blends white lobelia with harmonious blue and purple million bells for a hanging basket that's full of movement.

🅐 Euphorbia 'Diamond Frost'

Euphorbia hybrid; diamond frost

Gorgeous and graceful wherever it goes, euphorbia never fails to delight with its soaring delicacy and tenacious growth habit. It will love the heat at the top of the basket, while the bacopa (which prefers slightly cooler temperatures) enjoys being shaded far below.

🅑 Lobelia 'Laguna White'

Lobelia erinus; Indian tobacco

'Laguna White' isn't the old-fashioned lobelia. Its robust garden performance and airy habit make it perfect for designs, and it harmonizes perfectly with 'Diamond Frost' euphorbia.

🅒 Petunia 'Supertunia White'

Petunia x *hybrida;* trailing petunia

Supertunias can have many different moods depending on the colour. When the white catches the sun, it's so bright that it's almost translucent. If you aren't fertilizing this basket enough, the Supertunias will tell you with pale green leaves.

🅓 Bacopa 'Snowstorm'

see p. 120

Designing with 'Snow Princess'

'Snow Princess' lobularia deserves a mention here. It's an alyssum that has been recently hybridized to be more heat tolerant and to trail prolifically. It might not look very appealing at the garden centre in May, but as you can see it becomes gorgeous in summer. I took this picture outside Salisbury on August 15, and it had been glorious since the middle of June (photo A).

A (bottom left); B (above)

The human eye sees through context. A design that is one colour/texture/size has no sense of scale because we have nothing to compare it with. Add some trailing verbena to your 'Snow Princess,' and like a few black sheep in a white herd, suddenly the scale and measure make sense, and it looks more like a design and less like an undifferentiated mountain snow storm (photo B).

The only thing to be wary about with 'Snow Princess' is that it will make a mess of white petals underneath it, so keep that in mind when you are thinking about where to hang the basket or place the container in which it's planted.

Height: to 1.2 m • **Spread:** to 80 cm

MEG AND I FOUND this stunning basket hanging outside a cafe in old town Quebec. It's a gorgeous recipe that uses multiple colour contrasts to get a second look from anyone and everyone strolling by on a summer's day. All of the contrasts make it dynamic to look at, and if it can grab my attention on one of the busiest tourist streets in Canada, think about the attention it will grab in your yard!

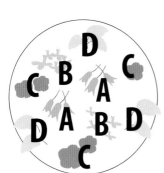

Ⓐ Begonia 'Million Kisses'

Ⓑ Lobelia 'Laguna Sky Blue'

Ⓒ Calibrachoa 'Superbells Tequila Sunrise'

Ⓓ Lamium

Recommended container size:
40–55 cm across

This design uses multiple complementary colours that dazzle the eye simultaneously. The red begonia flowers contrast sharply with their green foliage, and the blue lobelia clashes against the orange calibrachoa. On top of the contrasting colours are the contrasting shapes of the flowers, from the wickedly tubular begonias to the rounded calibrachoa.

This basket would be ideal for a partial sun or, because it's the sun-loving begonias, even full sun area in the yard. Try not to let it dry out too much because the begonias aren't very drought tolerant, and when you water it, soak the leaves with the nozzle sprayer (especially in drier areas) to increase the humidity around the container.

Upon closer inspection, I saw that the container was a wire basket, with the calibrachoa and lamium planted into the moss. If you want to add

a sense of height to your hanging basket to give it extra presence, a moss-lined basket is a good tactic (although I would have planted the calibrachoa on top and the begonias below to correspond better with their preferred moisture levels).

Many North Vancouver streets are lined with summer baskets featuring triad colour schemes.

A Begonia 'Million Kisses'

Begonia x *hybrida;* trailing begonia

Fairly new but very impressive, sun-loving, trailing begonias can take full sun (if tempered with a little humidity, either from the air or from the hose) and grow quickly to fill out a basket. The vivid, reddish pink flowers are a stark contrast with the dark green leaves.

B Lobelia 'Laguna Sky Blue'

Lobelia erinus; Indian tobacco

The calming blue of the lobelia keeps the basket from becoming too loud. It also contrasts with the orange million bells. Lobelia's sparse growth habit allows it to intersperse with the begonias so that the reddish pink and blue sprinkle together.

C Calibrachoa 'Superbells Tequila Sunrise'

Calibrachoa hybrid; million bells

These flowers are always beautiful and reliable! If you hang this basket in a partly shady spot, don't be shy about giving the million bells a generous haircut when they start to get leggy. With ample fertilizer, they will be back and brilliant in no time.

D Lamium

see p. 252

Making BIG Hanging Baskets

Creating hanging baskets that have a full-bodied appeal and look like they belong on a cobblestone street isn't as hard as you may think. The first step, of course, is to find a suitable moss basket frame to use. Look for one that is at least 40 centimetres in diameter (the bigger the better), and make sure it has a sturdy metal chain hanger. I don't suggest plastic because once the plants are mature and you're watering it, there's going to be a lot of weight.

A (bottom left); B (above)

When you're going for big colour, you need to start with big ingredients. Check the tags before you buy to make sure your chosen plants are aggressive varieties that will grow large. Forget about plants that play nice; to get a really big show, you want plants that will be constantly struggling against each other. In one of the baskets we found in Quebec City, the aggressive alternanthera had almost completely devoured some of its less-aggressive container-mates (photo A). If this starts to happen to your design, you can save the passive plant with your scissors or sit back and watch the show—in this case, the latter was much more impressive!

We found amazing boulevard baskets on the Victoria harbour that used bold, primary-coloured plants including schizanthus, bidens and lobelia to really make an impression (photo B).

Eruption in Moss

Height: to 1.5 m • **Spread:** to 70 cm

MEG FOUND THIS spectacular moss basket hanging outside a restaurant, and I just had to include it. Sometimes you have to just sit back and admire a composition that throws subtlety out the window to become a visual smorgasbord of colour! More of a planting style than a recipe, I recommend this one for anyone who wants to inject a potent dose of highly caffeinated colour into their yard. One look and you can't help but smile at the raw enthusiasm of so many flowers embracing the world.

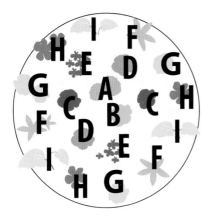

Recommended container size:
50–70 cm across

Ⓐ Begonia 'Non-Stop Red' and
Ⓑ 'Non-Stop Yellow'

Ⓒ Calibrachoa 'Superbells Red' and
Ⓓ 'Superbells Tequila Sunrise'

Ⓔ Lobelia 'Laguna Compact Blue with Eye'

Ⓕ Campanula 'Blue Waterfall'

Ⓖ Mecardonia 'Goldflake'

Ⓗ Bacopa 'Snowstorm'

Ⓘ Lamium

This basket is an excellent example of a triad colour scheme. Yellow, red and blue are side by side and create a vibrant sense of colour without a lot of blaring contrast. These colours aren't combative with each other; they simply celebrate their pure hues.

Although it doesn't seem like it at first, there is a method to this blooming madness. The thriller is planted into the top of the basket. Because this basket is hanging on a shady wall, it's three 'Non-Stop' begonias, but it could just as easily be 'Soprano' osteospermums or (if you want more vertical appeal) gaura or purple fountain grass.

Below the begonias, the fillers and spillers are planted in tiers, with the sun lovers and more drought-tolerant plants (calibrachoa and lobelia) on top and annuals that can take some shelter and/or need to stay moist

(bacopa, campanula and lamium) toward the bottom.

After you line the basket with moss, put it on a small pedestal and move around it in circles, planting each tier from the bottom up, layering them as if you were laying shingles. Leave enough room between them for the plants to grow in so the basket is full and radiant in a few weeks. You can save money by using annuals in packs (violas, milliflora petunias, lobelia) as long as you plant them close together.

'Non-Stop' begonias still bring the brightest and most honestly exuberant colour to the shadiest spots in the garden.

Ⓐ Begonia 'Non-Stop Red'
Ⓑ and 'Non-Stop Yellow'

Begonia x *tuberhybrida;* tuberous begonia

'Non-Stops' have survived the test of time and continue to light up the nooks of our yards with colour. Let the surface of the soil dry between waterings, and pinch off the single-blooming flowers.

Ⓒ Calibrachoa 'Superbells Red' and
Ⓓ 'Superbells Tequila Sunrise'

see p. 124

Ⓔ Lobelia 'Laguna Compact Blue with Eye'

see p. 128

Ⓕ Campanula 'Blue Waterfall'

Campanula poscharskyana; Serbian bellflower

This relatively new stuffer really impresses with a shower of star-shaped, sky blue flowers hanging down in thick sheets. After its first flush, cut it back gently and you may get another in early fall when the weather cools a little.

Ⓖ Mecardonia 'Goldflake'

see p. 296

Ⓗ Bacopa 'Snowstorm'

Sutera cordata; water hyssop

Bacopa hangs below everything else in long strands of white flowers. Use it at the bottom because bacopa needs to be kept moist or its flowers and buds will dry up and you'll have nothing but green for a month or so.

Ⓘ Lamium

see p. 252

BIG Colour

If you want to make a big impression, why not make a really big one? You can make a moss basket as large as you can get a metal assembly for it (if you can't find a premade one large enough, a welder will be able to

A (above); B (below)

make one for you that will last a life-time). Simply layer the moss into the assembly and fill it with soil as you go. Work your way up, laying plants down in layers and then adding more moss and soil on top of them until you reach the top, trying to save the most drought-tolerant plants for the top layers.

Meg and I found some massive moss planters at a cafe in a small Quebec town (photo B). Make sure your hanger and bracket can support a lot of weight if you want to make your moss hangers this large!

Of course, I have to mention the plant towers that I see from time to time. The ones pictured are impatiens and were grown in Vancouver (photo A). In Ontario I've seen them made of 'Wave' petunias, with the same incredible effect. They are actually

quite easy to care for and are basically large, metal trees with holders for dozens of pots. The pots are filled with plants, stacked up, irrigated with some tubes and voila! If you're interested in making one, call a large garden centre and they may be able to point you in the right direction.

Margarita

Height: to 1 m • **Spread:** to 90 cm

USING SIMILAR ELEMENTS around a sitting area condenses the space, pulling it together in a way that relaxes the eye and invites the visitor into the midst of the harmony. These fairly simple recipes work best when used together around one area. Even though they are vibrant, energetic colours, their shapes harmonize enough with each other to make the scene soothing, their warm tones inviting you to sink into a chair and watch their blooms glow in the sunlight.

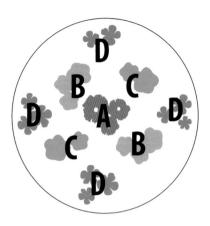

A Petunia 'Supertunia Royal Magenta'

B Calibrachoa 'Superbells Apricot Punch'

C Calibrachoa 'Superbells Tequila Sunrise'

D Bacopa 'Snowstorm'

Recommended container size:
25–35 cm across

This grouping works because the plants are different enough to be interesting but have enough recurring colours and shapes that they blend almost seamlessly together. I arranged this grouping as an example to show you the principle of using varied repetition to define a space. Don't be afraid to substitute widely and freely, using harmonizing shapes and textures and similar colour themes (but different enough that they aren't completely repeating each other) around your favourite outdoor sitting area.

The containers in the grouping need not all be hanging baskets, either; you can easily incorporate a window box or patio container into the mix, perhaps introducing a vertical element like a grass into one of them.

As long as you have a sunny spot and some fertilizer, this composition is foolproof. The ingredients are readily available and easy to take care of, and they grow well together. In humid regions where petunias and calibrachoa don't grow as well, try the warm tones of trailing begonias—mixing the big flowers of Illumination Series with the jagged, bountiful flowers of sun-loving 'Million Kisses' or 'Bellagio' will be beautiful.

This hanging basket excites the eye thanks to the zesty colours it uses.

ⒶPetunia 'Supertunia Royal Magenta'

Petunia x *hybrida*; trailing petunia

One of the most popular annuals in drier regions, 'Royal Magenta' is a rich, warm purple that intrigues the eye as it intensifies to ultraviolet in the centre. Closely related to million bells but not as drought tolerant, petunias' large, round flowers provide a little variety to the size of flower while still providing harmony.

ⒷCalibrachoa 'Superbells Apricot Punch'
Ⓒand 'Superbells Tequila Sunrise'

Calibrachoa hybrids; million bells

Some of the most versatile annuals I've encountered, million bells are almost maintenance free and have a naturally compact, free-blooming habit that will make you look like a pro (even if you're not—wink, wink). If the summer is cool and wet, they will start to get leggy. Trim them back and hope for warmer, drier days in September.

ⒹBacopa 'Snowstorm'

see p. 120

Using Warm Colours

For many of us, the patio, deck or garden is our retreat after a long day in the rat race. It's a place of solace that nurtures as we nurture it, as if the effort we pour into it to make it our own is an investment of energy that the space will return to us when we're exhausted and need energy the most.

The easiest way to create a feeling of relaxation in your outdoor living space is to incorporate a warm palette into your designs. Rich harmonies of oranges, coppers, yellows, reds and browns are always soothing. Some of the most reliable ingredients to use to create a relaxing colour scheme are

A (bottom left); B (above)

richly coloured grasses, like sedge, and orange calibrachoa (photo B).

Orange osteospermums and rust-coloured coleus are other relaxing ingredients that are easy to track down and take care of (photo A). Osteos tend to bloom in flushes, so make sure to give them a slight haircut after each flush to get them blooming again sooner.

If you want to incorporate warm colours into your yard, I suggest a grouping of containers around where you like to decompress. If your warm design gets leggy in mid-summer, give it a gentle pinch. At the end of August when the new flush of flowers comes, it will look as if you designed it just for the fall season.

Height: to 80 cm • **Spread:** to 80 cm

CONTAINER GARDENING is about so much more than creating loud, energetic compositions. Sometimes relaxation and simplicity are golden, especially when they're close to the sitting area where you go to unwind with a chardonnay and a good book at the end of the day. This recipe is probably the most calming one I've seen this year. It's the perfect colour scheme to soothe the nerves, with oceanic blue lobelia lapping against a soft chiffon million bells beach.

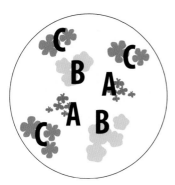

Ⓐ Lobelia 'Laguna Compact Blue with Eye'

Ⓑ Calibrachoa 'Superbells Yellow Chiffon'

Ⓒ Bacopa 'Snowstorm'

Recommended container size:
25–35 cm across

If you want to get the most out of the calming effects of this composition, arrange a grouping of containers, whether it's hanging baskets, patio pots or window boxes, with these ingredients around your sitting area. The recipe is easy enough to substitute freely within it. To use it in a patio pot, consider a 'Pony Tail' stipa grass in the centre, rising out of the lobelia, where it can sway in the breeze and add yet another calming element.

When you create groupings of containers, try to think in odd numbers (in threes if possible). An odd number of pots is just off-balance enough to create a small amount of visual tension and interest. The exception, of course, is when you are deliberately framing both sides of a focal point, like a doorway.

The ingredients here are easy to find and almost maintenance free. If the million bells get leggy during wet, cloudy spells, cut them back and they will bloom lavishly as soon as the sun comes out again. Make sure the container is in a sunny spot and be generous with the fertilizer; these are high-performance ingredients.

Yellow Supertunias blend well with purple Superbells to create a contrasting basket that, thanks to its ability to catch sunlight, is still quite soothing.

Ⓐ Lobelia 'Laguna Compact Blue with Eye'
Lobelia erinus; Indian tobacco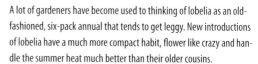

A lot of gardeners have become used to thinking of lobelia as an old-fashioned, six-pack annual that tends to get leggy. New introductions of lobelia have a much more compact habit, flower like crazy and handle the summer heat much better than their older cousins.

Ⓑ Calibrachoa 'Superbells Yellow Chiffon'
Calibrachoa hybrid; million bells

This fairly new colour is a deliciously subtle yellow, and we've found that it's been very versatile in baskets and containers. It keeps its habit and blooms as much as other Superbells, which are starting to usurp the mighty Supertunia as the container stuffer of choice in drier regions.

Ⓒ Bacopa 'Snowstorm'
see p. 120

Designing with Calibrachoa

Calibrachoa, which is usually known as million bells, the ubiquitous Proven Winners brand name, is becoming one of the most popular annuals across Canada. At Salisbury we grow more and more of it every year, from small pots to hanging baskets to large mixed containers. It's related to petunias but is more drought resistant (making it easier for

A (bottom left); B (above)

enclosed containers) and more forgiving of humid climates than petunias. And, perhaps most importantly, it no longer has that nasty stickiness that gets all over your hands!

The number of colours of million bells available is beginning to border on the ridiculous, with ever more colours coming out every year. Make sure you choose plants that are well branching. I've found the Superbells

Series to be the most reliable, but growth habits are often a matter of personal taste. One of my favourites is 'Superbells Plum' (photo A).

Trailing petunias (Supertunia Series) are a natural match with million bells even though they have slightly different watering preferences. In hanging baskets, the different sizes of flowers with the same round shape make an intriguing combination (photo B).

Suncatcher

Height: to 1.2 m • **Spread:** to 70 cm

COLOURS ARE BUILT of light, and they change their moods depending on the light conditions they're in. Yellow and purple react to light especially dramatically, their moods going from dour and brooding in low light to elated in high light. This basket is exceptional in the way it reacts to light. When it catches the afternoon sun, the yellow Supertunias become almost translucent and the lilac shades underneath begin to pulse with life.

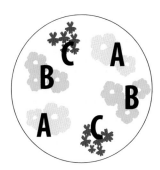

A Petunia 'Wave Misty Lilac'

B Petunia 'Supertunia Citrus'

C Verbena 'Superbena Large Lilac Blue'

Recommended container size:
30–40 cm across

The ingredients here are simple, but they are carefully chosen. There are no striking contrasts or clashes of colour. The soft pastels relax the eye, and the shapes of the flowers and leaves are different enough to provide variety but not enough to break the sense of calm that the recipe creates. This combination is for a lazy summer's day spent with lemonade and an engrossing novel.

The petunias are light enough that the sun will shine through them, lighting them up and making the whole basket glow. Put this container in an exposed area where you can appreciate its different moods and watch it catch the light at numerous times during the day. In the morning the fresh light will awaken them, and by afternoon the petals will seem to be on fire. In the evening the softening twilight will turn them a warm hue, especially the yellow.

This recipe is planted in a regular plastic hanging basket and would be perfect in drier regions where moss tends to dry out quickly. Petunias and verbena love basking in the sun. If the summer turns cloudy and cool, they will get leggy and pale; don't be afraid to cut them back and fertilize, and they will grow back when the heat returns. If you want something more drought tolerant, look for light shades of calibrachoa.

Yellow Supertunias have the most sparkling relationship with colour of any plant I've seen.

ⓐ Petunia 'Wave Misty Lilac'

Petunia x *hybrida;* trailing petunia

Although often overlooked for flashier colours, 'Wave Misty Lilac' has an excellent habit and blooms all summer. Its soothing tones are best matched with other calming pastels.

ⓑ Petunia 'Supertunia Citrus'

Petunia x *hybrida;* trailing petunia

A 'Supertunia Citrus' is a little like a black pansy; it took a lot of fancy science to get here. 'Citrus' is popular both because it is unique and because it has a nice habit in a hanging basket. Like all Supertunias, it doesn't like to dry out and needs full sun.

ⓒ Verbena 'Superbena Large Lilac Blue'

Verbena x *hybrida;* trailing verbena

Old-fashioned varieties of verbena have often been slow growing and reluctant to bloom. Varieties bred for use in container gardening, like the Superbena Series, are remarkably prolific and colourful. Keep it on the dry side, fertilize it generously and it will produce vibrant colour all summer.

Harnessing Light

Different colours are just different variations of light, and how your design interacts with light at different times of day will determine how you see it. White, yellow and some lilac tones tend to reflect light, making them very cheery additions to sunny spots. Silver flowers are sometimes called "daylight extenders" because they absorb light during the day and give off a subtle glow after twilight, like solar panels. Darker colours, such as burgundy, deep red and purple, will absorb light, often giving them a deep presence in the garden that can border on brooding.

A (bottom left); B (above)

I remember seeing the work of the great Impressionists in Paris and being in awe of how they used light and shadow to create such vivid emotions. My wife Meg, inspired by their work, uses light to stunning effect in her paintings. When I saw this container, I automatically thought of her and the Impressionists (photo A).

'Supertunia Citrus' petunia is one of the most "Impressionist" flowers thanks to its ability to reflect light and become almost luminescent. Combine it with lime sweet potato vine for a vivid and cheerful basket (photo B).

Quetzal

Height: to 1.2 m • **Spread:** to 70 cm

THE FIRST TIME I saw this basket I thought of a jellyfish, hovering close to the surface of the water while its tendrils sweep in lazy but deliberate arcs below it, looking for unsuspecting critters. It's a treat to look at, with its bulging mushroom of tropical colour at the top and the curving, silver vines below. More than many other hanging baskets, this one seems like it's meant to be floating in space, giving it a refreshingly buoyant feeling.

A New Guinea impatiens

B Lotus vine

C Begonia 'Million Kisses'

Recommended container size:
35–50 cm across

This recipe uses the shapes of the ingredients in a playful way. While the New Guinea impatiens grow into a well-defined bell shape, the lotus vine arc downward, almost like a fern would. The designer has sprinkled some trailing begonias into the mix as well, to add some spicy colour to the vines.

The "flying saucer effect" here is created by using a bell-shaped, colourful annual over hanging vines. You can experiment freely within this design by substituting other annuals (not just impatiens) and other vines. For this design in the shade, mounding petunias and English ivy would work well.

Moss baskets have seen a burst of popularity in the last decade, especially in humid regions. They are surprisingly easy to make even though they look difficult. If you live in a dry region you can still enjoy moss baskets, but they will need a little extra care. When you water the plants, make sure to soak the moss as well. Moss is a sponge,

so the more moisture it absorbs, the more humid it makes the air for the tropical plants around it.

'Pink Marshmallow' fuchsia is a reliable shade plant that grows straight down and blooms all summer as long as it is fertilized.

Ⓐ New Guinea impatiens
Impatiens x *hawkeri;* busy Lizzie

Their bell-shaped growth habit makes them perfect for this design. You can use any colour you like—they are all rich and tropical. Make sure they stay moist, and protect them from the afternoon sun if you are in a dry region.

Ⓑ Lotus vine
Lotus berthelotii; parrot's beak

Although it's still rare in designing, this little plant has become more popular in the last couple of years. It's easy to care for and handles many exposures, and its delicate, silvery vines have tremendous design potential. It takes a while to bloom, but when it does, its flowers are exquisitely shaped.

Ⓒ Begonia 'Million Kisses'
see p. 116

Shade Containers

Even though there aren't as many design options for the shade, you still have a lot of room to play and experiment with shade plants. Most of the high-performance annuals being released these days are for sunny spots. One great way to dramatically expand your choice of ingredients to use in the shade is to look at plants typically used inside

A (bottom left); B (above)

the house. Since most houseplants do well in partial shade or full shade, think of the houseplant section of the garden centre as up for grabs when it comes to making designs for the shade.

When you have a complicated recipe with many elements of design at play, it's often a good idea to pair it with a much simpler, harmonious container. Doing so will give the eye a chance to rest on the simplicity after being stimulated by the complexity. The feature container ("Quetzal") was actually part of a line of containers at Butchart Gardens outside Victoria. The baskets alternated between the feature and large baskets of tradescantia, a traditional houseplant that does best in partial sun but will tolerate shade. The effect was impressive; the simpler container soothed the eye while the complicated container excited it, providing a great sense of balance overall (photo A).

Mario Salazar, our head grower, designed a simple shade container to sit atop his hosta bed. He chose 'Illumination' trailing begonias and some soft green oxalis to create a cool-coloured, woodland design that harmonized well with the hostas below (photo B).

Devonian Postcards

Height: to 80 cm · **Spread:** to 60 cm

IT'S A CHALLENGE to find the perfect recipe for that area of the garden that receives almost no sun, as most new container stuffers are for high light. We found these baskets in Minter Gardens, outside Vancouver, and fell in love with them for their simplicity and adaptability. While the fern provides lush foliage and classic, even nostalgic beauty, the impatiens peek out from between its overhanging fronds, sprinkling the recipe with colour and giving it a slightly wild, rainforest appeal.

A Boston fern

B Impatiens 'Super Elfin'

C Vinca 'Wojo's Jem'

Recommended container size:
   35–55 cm across

Boston ferns have been around for hundreds of years and are one of the most popular houseplants in the world. They will thrive in a moss basket in the shade, especially if you spray down the moss and the foliage when you water to keep the humidity up. The sphagnum acts as a sponge, wicking moisture but then increasing the relative humidity around it as it dries. The fern will also grow into the moss, creating the illusion that you've planted ferns in the moss when you haven't.

The most impressive thing about these containers is that they are more of a template than a recipe. You have a large fern, a shade-loving, flowering annual, and a shade-loving vine. Within that basic formula you're free to substitute widely according to your taste.

If you want something trendier than a Boston fern, try a leatherleaf fern or a Japanese painted fern with beautifully tinged leaves. If single impatiens aren't for you, try trailing begonias for a big impact, or bronze-leafed fibrous begonias for their built-in contrast. If you have morning light then you might want to try violas in the moss basket. Using this recipe as a starting point, you can customize a basket to fit your shady nook perfectly.

Ferns can provide a stately and elegantly Victorian touch to the garden.

A Boston fern

Nephrolepis exaltata; sword fern

Easy to find and easy to take care of, Bostons prefer sheltered (or indirect) light and to be always kept moist, or they will shed. They don't need as much fertilizer as many other annuals, but a little will keep the fronds a rich green. There are good substitutions you can make if you're not quite sold on a Boston fern.

B Impatiens 'Super Elfin'

Impatiens walleriana; busy Lizzie

'Super Elfin' is slightly shorter and more compact than the Accent Series, making it ideal for moss baskets. If it gets too leggy, don't be shy about cutting it back.

C Vinca 'Wojo's Jem'

Vinca major; periwinkle

Vinca is a classic vine that boasts slightly glossy, creamy white leaves with dark green edges. Vinca is easy to grow and hangs in straight, vertical lines, which makes it ideal for many types of designs.

A (above)

Staple Plants for the Shade

Ferns are enjoying a renaissance as savvy gardeners are discovering their adaptability into countless design styles. A simple Boston fern, English ivy combination creates an easy, classical, refreshing (Bostons are one of the top air-cleaning plants in the world) composition (photo A).

Wherever ferns go, they take their sense of ancient, rugged beauty with them, so keep that in mind when you use them. Put a small Boston in a mixed hanging basket with lobelia and torenia, and it instantly adds a prehistoric "oomph" to the otherwise gentle container (photo B).

B (above); C (below)

Recognizing the psychological associations that we have with some plants will allow you as the designer to use those associations to your benefit.

Fuchsia is another shade-loving staple that's being rediscovered for its versatility, though it's not enjoying quite the same burst of excitement surrounding ferns. One of the most easily recognizable and beautiful shade plants around, its pendulous blooms hang like vibrant, bulging insects, making it a gorgeous addition to any shade container (photo C).

Prairie Breezes

Height: to 1 m • **Spread:** to 1 m

WE DISCOVERED THIS showstopper on a boulevard, and it would make a big impact in your garden. The recipe is simple and doesn't get fancy with architecture or textures; it's about big, colourful plants billowing out of the container in blooms of pure colour. Use this container to pull the eye wherever you want it to be, whether that's to the outdoor living area or to the centre of the yard. Thanks to its complete and utter lack of subtlety, you will be able to put it a long way from your living area and still enjoy it.

A Purple fountain grass

B Black-eyed Susan 'Tiger Eye'

C Calibrachoa 'Superbells Blue'

D Calibrachoa 'Superbells Lavender'

Recommended container size:
  50–70 cm across

The two most musical phrases to a gardener's ear are "simple to put together" and "easy to take care of." This recipe isn't fussy; just role your sleeves up and cram in the colour. The complementary colour scheme of the orange and blue is very simple. You can choose any complementary colours and get the same effect, so feel free to substitute freely.

If you want a harmonious container, try orange or red calibrachoa instead of blue. You can also try a vine-like lysimachia if you want more trailing appeal. If you really want to stir things up, plunk a large shrub, such as a maple, into the centre instead of the fountain grass. The fountain grass is there to provide a bit of texture and vertical appeal to keep the design from becoming completely shapeless.

If you showcase this design in a corner of your garden where people don't normally go, it just might intrigue them enough to take the walk over. Put it in full sun (the hotter the better) and fertilize it liberally. You shouldn't need to rescue anything; the growth habits are varied enough that they won't grow together.

Almost any combination of black-eyed Susan and fountain grass will give you a gorgeous container. Here, the designer has added sweet potato vine for foliage.

A Purple fountain grass
Pennisetum setaceum

Although this container doesn't emphasize texture or vertical appeal, without the fountain grass it would just look like a mass of colour. The sun-loving grass rescues it from shapelessness by adding something other than colour to entertain the eye. The way the feathery plumes catch the wind is wonderful to watch.

B Black-eyed Susan 'Tiger Eye'
Rudbeckia hirta; gloriosa daisy

Relatively new to the gardening world, 'Tiger Eye' is an exceptional black-eyed Susan that performs beautifully all summer without the characteristic raggedy foliage that goes along with most other black-eyed Susans. Big, bright yellow flowers bursting into the sun—what more could you ask for?

C Calibrachoa 'Superbells Blue' and
D 'Superbells Lavender'
Calibrachoa hybrids; million bells

Planting million bells is one of the best ways there is to look like a gardening genius. They grow like crazy in full sun and are at their best in containers that throw subtlety out the window and are all about big colour.

A (above)

Prairie-themed Designs

Black-eyed Susans and grasses are refreshingly reliable ingredients that, when used together, are certain to bring with them feelings of long, lingering summer days and big Prairie skies stretching from horizon to horizon. The grasses catch every good breeze while the black-eyed Susans seem to worship the sun with their broad, exuberant blooms (photo A).

There are many sizes and colours of *Rudbeckia* with a steady flow of new introductions, from the tiny, container-stuffing 'Toto' to the massive 'Prairie

B (above); C (below)

Sun.' 'Tiger Eye' is one of the best introductions I've seen, and I recommend it for containers thanks to its compact habit and free-blooming style (photo B).

Grasses are available in every shape and size as well! One of my favourites, besides the always reliable purple fountain grass, is the airy, breeze-catching stipa (photo C). Another favourite is 'Bunny Tail', which is a dwarf version of the larger fountain grass and, if I may say so, much cuter than its big brother.

Canadian Afternoon

Height: 50 cm • **Spread:** to 2 m

MY MOTHER IS an excellent example of the balance that many savvy gardeners have struck between the excitement of modernity and the comfort of tradition. Always curious and eager to try new things, she's always asking me what's new and interesting. However, she doesn't see why she should abandon plants that she's loved for decades, like geraniums, just because they aren't trendy anymore. This recipe is from her garden and is a gorgeous example of how making modern designs doesn't have to mean sacrificing the plants you grew up with.

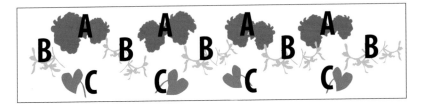

Ⓐ Zonal geranium

Ⓑ Euphorbia 'Diamond Frost'

Ⓒ Sweet potato vine 'Sweet Caroline Purple'

Recommended container size:
30 cm by 90 cm

This photo shows a hot row of window boxes with south and east exposure. The geraniums, of course, are her favourite; they stay the same every year and always look fantastic. The lacy billows of euphorbia will drift in between the geranium flower stalks to give the appearance of red clusters floating on a white cloud. Red and white together has a powerful effect on me wherever I see it.

Come Canada Day, there is no better design with which to celebrate. It showcases our patriotic colours and also illustrates the balance between tradition and modernity that many Canadian gardeners think about every spring.

The sweet potato vine will grow quickly in the summer heat as long as it's well fertilized. If you want to add a little more textural excitement, use the new, highly serrated Illusion Series. If you want to take it a step further into the contemporary, ask for 'Fireworks' geraniums, which have wickedly pointed flowers that would blend dramatically with the euphorbia.

Red-tinged 'Blush' euphorbia blends perfectly with red Superbells.

Ⓐ Zonal geranium

Pelargonium x *hortorum*

Whether in Grandma's or Mom's garden, we all grew up with geraniums. They're one of the easiest annuals across Canada to find and take care of, and as long as you deadhead them when they're done blooming, they will delight all summer long.

Ⓑ Euphorbia 'Diamond Frost'

Euphorbia hybrid; diamond frost

This variety is one of the most successful introductions in the past few years, and more varieties of euphorbia are being introduced all the time. I've found 'Diamond Frost' to boast the best balance of flower-power and semi-compact habit. There is a red euphorbia in the Blush Series that would harmonize a little more with the geraniums. Euphorbia is so, so easy as long as you water occasionally and fertilize generously.

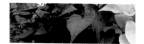

Ⓒ Sweet potato vine 'Sweet Caroline Purple'
see p. 92

Designing for Canada

We live in the best country in the world, and luckily, our flag has such a simple and versatile colour scheme that it's simple to create designs that celebrate Canada. Although we don't flaunt it very much, we love our country intensely and I'm always delighted to see how Canadians embrace the flag's colours when they have the chance (photo B).

When you are making a Canadian design, there are only a few rules of

A (bottom left); B (above)

thumb to remember. One is to try to keep the red as close to the flag's red as possible; otherwise it just won't look like the flag. Another is to try to keep the red central and the white supplemental. On the flag, the red maple leaf is the central aspect and is set upon the white backdrop. On my mom's feature window boxes, the geraniums are the central aspect and the euphorbia acts as the backdrop, thus keeping the emphasis the same as the flag.

The great thing about Canadian-themed designs is that the bigger and bolder you are, the more people will love it. At Minter Gardens outside Vancouver we found a massive flag made out of fibrous begonias (photo A). I used to fill the big roadside sign at Salisbury with hundreds of red and white geraniums, and people driving by would call later to comment on how much they enjoyed it.

Vanilla and Spice

Height: to 70 cm • **Spread:** to 60 cm

THIS CALMING CONTAINER brings a feel of the cottage with it, blending soft greens and relaxing blues in an informal collage. There's a lovely sense of nostalgia with this one, a gentle warmth that comes from the blend of its various smells, rugged textures and an informal sense of line throughout. It's a perfect recipe to experiment with, as well. If you have a soft-spoken plant that has always brought a smile to your face, this is the place to try it.

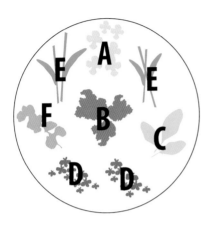

Ⓐ Angelonia 'Angelface White'

Ⓑ Heliotrope 'Atlantis'

Ⓒ Golden leaf sage

Ⓓ Lobelia 'Laguna Compact Blue with Eye'

Ⓔ Sweet flag

Ⓕ Licorice plant 'Licorice Splash'

Recommended container size:
30–40 cm across

There is a mix of traditional ingredients with newer ones here. The golden leaf sage contributes its soft sandpaper texture, and the licorice plant provides some foliage. The lobelia, heliotrope and angelonia add colour that never gets too vibrant or outspoken for a lazy day in the hammock. The heliotrope also adds its vanilla perfume.

While it's neither a stirring focal point nor the container to give the best spot around your sitting area to, this recipe should be in a high-traffic area where the heliotrope smell can ambush people walking by. Part of its appeal is that it is an ensemble piece, with no one ingredient playing the prima donna. The heliotrope has the role of getting your attention, the sage has the role of getting your hands involved and the sweet flag and the angelonia have the role of framing the scene with a hint of verticality.

Cottage-themed containers go nicely with folksy garden statues and figurines, so don't be bashful about using them together.

Ⓐ Angelonia 'Angelface White'
Angelonia angustifolia; summer snapdragon

Angelonia is one of those intriguing newer annuals that looks like it's been around for a hundred years. It blooms sequentially up the vertical stems. Although it's probably not going to stop traffic, it's often the right ingredient to add a sense of thrill to a medium-sized container. Keep it in full sun.

Ⓑ Heliotrope 'Atlantis'
Heliotropium arborescens; cherry pie

Heliotrope is beloved for its rich vanilla scent. Named after Helios, god of the sun, it loves exposed spots but in drier regions will still need some protection from the afternoon sun—watch for burning on the leaves. It has somewhat finicky watering needs and wants to dry out slightly between waterings.

Ⓒ Golden leaf sage
Salvia officinalis

One of the "designer" sages, its touchable leaves are tinged with a soft green variegation. Sage has one of the most recognizable scents of any plant, and you'll catch people rubbing it softly between their fingertips to catch a bit of that classic smell.

Ⓓ Lobelia 'Laguna Compact Blue with Eye'
see p. 128

Ⓔ Sweet flag
Acorus calamus

Sweet flag is a marginal grass that performs well in container gardens if it's kept moist. If you have a very wet area in the garden it will do well there, as well. It's grown for its variegated foliage and sends out insignificant flowers in summer that won't get a second look.

Ⓕ Licorice plant 'Licorice Splash'
see p. 104

Cottage Designs

Although there's a rich and well-established tradition for "cottage" container gardens, there really isn't one tried and true way of designing

A (above left); B (above right)

one. The best way that I've found is to build your container with the idea of lazy summer days spent dozing at a lake cottage, reading a good book cover to cover. Cottage designing is more of a feeling than a formal style. Usually the ingredients used are fairly soft spoken and low maintenance, but they don't have to be old-fashioned.

Lynn Parker has some containers that would fit perfectly into a cottage theme. She uses simple, rustic cedar containers and cobbity daisies as her primary showpiece (photo A). Daisies have such a traditional feel to them that using them will add an instant warming nostalgia, and with newer varieties of daisies (such as cobbities), you don't have to sacrifice performance to get that feeling. Notice that in the daisy planter, as in the feature design ("Vanilla and Spice"), there is very little attention paid to architecture or contemporary line or texture; that's typical of cottage designs.

A simple herb container will often capture the feel of a cottage garden perfectly (photo B). Try to use classic, well-recognized herbs, and a touch of old-fashioned style (like marigolds to ward off the bugs) goes a long way!

Small-Town Pickets

Height: to 25 cm · **Spread:** to 30 cm

YOU DON'T HAVE to spend a lot of money on fancy containers. The more creative you are, the less you have to spend. Here is a great example of using found containers to make a big impact. The fescue, combined with the old-fashioned cottage feel of the brachyscome, creates a rustic, comfortable theme. Combine these elements with the simple repetition along the rural fence, and the scene in the picture looks like it could have been planted 70 years ago—perfect to create a little rough-around-the-edges nostalgia.

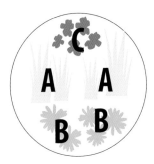

A Fescue 'Elijah Blue'

B Brachyscome 'Blue Zephyr'

C Nemesia 'Sky Blue Lagoon'

Recommended container size:
20–30 cm across

There are several layers of harmony at play here. The rough texture of the fescue emphasizes the rusty feel of the pails, while at first glance the subtle blue flowers might seem more like happily placed wildflowers than planned container stuffers.

If you use metal pails (or any metal), all you need to do is bang some holes in the bottom and line the container with a decent plastic. The lining will prevent toxins from the rust from leeching into the plant roots.

Pretty much any container you find has the potential to make a gorgeous container garden. The only catch is that you need to punch holes in the bottom for drainage (not so good if the container is a family heirloom). If it's a treated material that could be potentially toxic to sensitive roots, simply line it with plastic. Remember to leave proper drainage in the liner as well.

This recipe will be happiest in partial or full sun, but make sure the plants are kept well watered because the pails will get very hot during scorching afternoons. If they are going in an exposed spot, you may want to consider replacing the nemesia with something that revels in full sun, like 'Tukana Denim Blue' verbena or even an echeveria to add more architectural lines. If you want to add some contrast to the blue, mix in some coral-coloured portulaca. If you want to add more variety to the textural mix, try some 'Diamond Frost' euphorbia.

These Swan River daisies *(Brachyscome iberidifolia)* are both filler and spiller in this eye-catching, wall-mounted container.

A Fescue 'Elijah Blue'
Festuca glauca; blue fescue

Usually when we think of ornamental grasses we get fixated on fountain and pampas grasses, with their show-off plumes. What it lacks in size, soft-spoken blue fescue makes up for in its refreshing silver colour and irresistibly touchable spikiness. Hardy, easy and ruggedly handsome, fescue is like a cowboy who doesn't say much but really makes an impression.

B Brachyscome 'Blue Zephyr'
Brachyscome iberidifolia;
Swan River daisy

In stark contrast to their bountiful cobbity cousins, brachyscome daises are small, subtle and perfect in small containers. If they get leggy in wet, cloudy weather, just give them a haircut and they will bounce back when the sun returns.

C Nemesia 'Sky Blue Lagoon'
Nemesia fruticans

Nemesia is a cool-season gem that boasts dainty, cottage-garden flowers in early spring. It will make this design beautiful until the brachyscome starts to bloom in June. Keep it moist and pinch it back when the summer gets too hot for it.

Using Repetition Effectively

Repetition can be a very powerful tool for savvy garden designers to use. I already discussed the difference between varied repetition and simple repetition (see p. 68). Simple repetition can be very effective for a number of uses. In the feature design ("Small-Town Pickets"), the repeated elements work as an ideal mirror to the ubiquitous white pickets on the fence. If this design was to be used on a patio it may need to be varied in order to keep interest, but in the

A (bottom left); B (above)

context of this fence it's a perfect mood setter.

Repeated elements condense the space they're in, making them ideal for lining a path in the garden to soften it. The simple red petunia pots in photo A are visual stepping stones; the eye naturally skips from one to the other quickly to the end of the path at the other side.

Simple repetition can also be used vertically. It's common to find repeated pots lining the stairs leading up to a front door. Or, if you have a narrow spot, like a corner or alcove, and you want to fill it with colour, you can use a vertical plant stand with simple repeated pots to define the vertical space (photo B).

The Versailles Style

Size: depends on design

THE BRITISH AND French styles of garden design are two of the most well-known styles in history. If you compare the rustic, deliberately informal charm of St. James Park in London with the elegant and rigidly formal grounds at Versailles Palace, the difference becomes very clear. This bed, in Minter Gardens outside Vancouver, exemplifies the French style of well-defined beds and exquisite designs. This style, or a variation of it, wouldn't be difficult for you to incorporate into your own garden.

Recommended container size:
depends on design

As this bed was in an area that received a lot of shade, the primary flowers are 'Non-Stop' tuberous begonias and bronze-leafed fibrous begonias. The border of the beds is boxwood, which is an excellent staple hedging shrub in much of Canada (in cooler regions, cotoneaster is the best substitute). The carefully pruned boxwoods are laid out in a sharply angled yet curving design around the masses of pure colour.

French garden design isn't about subtle combinations. It's about using a plant's most apparent element of design en masse to create a vibrant display of pure colour and form. The small walkways are where lords walked with ladies in the afternoons, sheltering them from the sun with parasols. There's a nostalgic lavishness built into gardens like these, and after touring them through France it's nice to visit them in Canada.

You don't need to turn your yard into Versailles to incorporate the French style into your garden. All you have to do is enclose a grouping of annuals with some larger plants (the perimeter could be made up of any plants you want; it doesn't have to be shrubs) to create dramatic appeal.

The eye-popping effect comes from the mass of colour. French style is about taking one element of design and running with it. While our normal practice is to fill a bed with an assortment of perennials and annuals, the feature shows what it looks like to choose one plant and use it exclusively.

This breathtaking Roman-themed garden at Butchart reminded me that the possibilities are endless in garden design.

A Boxwood

Buxus sempervirens; European boxwood

Whenever I visit Europe, the boxwood in the gardens always greets me warmly and tells me where I am. It's that European flavour of boxwood that can make it so valuable to a designer. Planting it is a surefire way to create a British or French garden theme. Boxwood is only hardy in warm regions of Canada. Don't let it dry out too much.

B Cotoneaster

Cotoneaster spp.

If you don't live in a region warm enough for boxwoods to be hardy, then cotoneasters are a strong second choice. They are very popular shrubs across the prairies and can be pruned, given enough time, to be almost as thick and beautiful as their heat-loving counterparts. Cotoneasters produce red berries in fall that birds love to snack on.

Annuals in Flower Beds

When it comes to flower beds full of annuals, colour is king! If perennials beds are about vertical layers and big foliage, then annuals beds are about as many flowers blooming as possible. Unlike container gardens, in flower beds full of annuals, "thrillers" are rare and "spillers" are virtually non-existent. Flower beds are about "fillers" and making a big impression.

You don't need a trimmed boxwood border if you want to wow people with an annuals bed; all you need is

A (below)

The British gardening style is much more informal than the French style. It emphasizes lush perennials over manicured annuals.

C (below)

space. Take out a piece of lawn, usually in the front yard because an annuals bed is all about showing off, and backfill it with some soil with good drainage (or just add peat moss or another additive to increase the drainage of your black earth). You don't need high-performance, high-cost annuals for a bed. In fact, the cheaper pack-annuals tend to perform better in the ground (photo A).

You can be as simple or as elaborate as you want with annuals beds (photo C). For the front yard, I recommend keeping it simple; a block of colour stops traffic just as well as a professionally laid-out garden design. If you want even more impact, you could make a bed of just one type of annual, such as an African marigold.

Sweet Escapes

Height: to 2.5 m • **Spread:** to 1 m

LIKE MANY PEOPLE, I never really appreciated sweet peas. They were always just there, and I never looked at them as having any design potential; there was always something newer and more interesting. It wasn't until my wife re-introduced me to them that I began to look at them as having some real design potential, and now the more I use them, the more I like them! They are always more versatile than we give them credit for, so it's wonderful to see savvy gardeners start using them in containers.

Ⓐ Sweet pea

Recommended container size:
35–60 cm across

There are dozens of varieties of sweet peas available, from massive homesteader varieties to miniature designer types. I find that, despite all the hybridizing and science involved in producing the new varieties, the original types still have the strongest scent. The only exception that I've found is 'Cupid,' which is a relatively new, compact sweet pea, created for hanging baskets and container gardening, that boasts stunning aromas off soft pink blooms. The older varieties are easy to grow from seed, and I mean easy—throw some seeds in the container and you're done.

This container provides a simple pyramidal trellis for the vines to climb. As you can see, sweet peas will fill out a pot beautifully. If you want to add more variety to the mix, try planting some 'Laguna' lobelia or even 'Superbena' verbena, in your colour of choice, out the sides—just be prepared to protect either one from grasping sweet pea tendrils.

Sweet peas look good anywhere. If you put this container in the centre of the yard you'll have a beautiful centrepiece; if you keep it close to your sitting area you'll be able to smell the flowers. If you're a true sweet pea aficionado, make this container (with the homesteader variety) the centrepiece of a grouping of containers with an assortment of varieties. Remember that sweet peas will trail if you don't give them anything to grab on to, giving you another option to spice up your design.

Scarlet runner bean *(Phaseolus coccineus)* is another foolproof vine that grows like crazy from seed (and is delicious as a bonus).

Ⓐ **Sweet pea**
Lathyrus odoratus

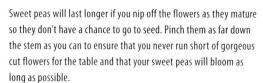

Sweet peas will last longer if you nip off the flowers as they mature so they don't have a chance to go to seed. Pinch them as far down the stem as you can to ensure that you never run short of gorgeous cut flowers for the table and that your sweet peas will bloom as long as possible.

The Underappreciated Gem

If you want to make the cheapest, easiest container in this book, here's what you should do. Get a large pot and a few sticks 1–1.5 metres long. Tie the sticks into a crude pyramid with fishing line and wrap the fishing line around and down the length of them. Then buy a bulk pack of sweet pea seeds and throw them in the soil around the sticks.

Keep the container well watered, and by late June or early July, the sweet peas will be in radiant bloom. The only maintenance is that you need to snip the flowers as they mature to prevent it going to seed, which stops blooming. Once blooming they are better enjoyed on the kitchen table anyway!

A (below); B (right)

Sweet peas have so much versatility in design that it surprises me that they are still considered an old-fashioned plant. Besides being the perfect thing to soften the look of a garden wall, they also thrive in containers because they are warmer there than in the ground. You can use them as climbing centrepieces or even trailing plants. Luella Chmelyk planted 'Cupid'

sweet peas in a small basket, and you couldn't miss the sweet aroma as you walked by (photo A).

Outside Salisbury, we planted sweet peas with some red fountain grass for a simple container that looked great (photo B). As long as they have nothing to climb up, they will cascade and bloom all summer.

The Untamed Canna

Height: to 1.2 m • **Spread:** to 90 cm

THIS COMBINATION is a classic "thriller, filler, spiller" that Meg and I found in a median planter at the Butchart Gardens near Victoria. Reliable and low maintenance, it's perfect for when the container or bed just has to look good. The rich wine reds of the canna lilies and New Guinea impatiens blend into a tropical harmony while the lobelia, trickling over the edges like tiny waterfalls, adds some intriguing contrast.

(A) Canna lily

(B) New Guinea impatiens 'Infinity Red'

(C) Lobelia 'Sapphire'

Recommended container size:
depends on design

You can make this recipe any size, from one canna in a container to dozens of them in a row in a bed. You can jazz it up by adding more elements to it, from curly willow stems to a mid-sized element like 'Red Shield' hibiscus or a barberry shrub, to fill the gap between the New Guineas and the cannas.

The established three-tiered rule of container design (thriller, filler, spiller) can also apply to beds. This recipe could easily be in a container, just as many container recipes could easily be planted into beds. The key differences between containers and beds are, one, that the soil is colder in beds so tropical species will have a sluggish start in the ground, and two, that beds tend to keep the roots more moist, so drought-loving plants such as succulents won't thrive in the ground as they will in containers.

The best thing about this recipe is that you can make almost endless

substitutions within the three-tiered approach. The cannas and New Guineas work well in humid parts of Canada, where New Guineas can be exposed to afternoon sunlight. In drier areas where the sun is hotter, try substituting a large grass, like millet or fountain grass, for the cannas and trailing petunias and calibrachoa for the New Guineas.

The sky is the limit for what you can do within this basic recipe. Stick to the established method and choose colours that you think blend well together, and you can't lose.

New Guinea impatiens bloom in rich, tropical colours that make them perfect for pairing with canna lilies.

Ⓐ **Canna lily**

Canna indica; Indian shot

Many people are surprised to see canna lilies planted in beds. Endlessly versatile, they thrive almost anywhere with some sun and fertilizer. Try them as a backdrop for one of your flower beds, perhaps instead of an established favourite like hollyhock, to bring some tropical flair into your yard. They are expensive, but you can easily transform them from annual to perennial by cutting them back after the first frost and digging up the bulb. Keep it cool and dry over winter as you would a potato (just don't put it in your stew), and it will come back even larger the next year.

Ⓑ **New Guinea impatiens 'Infinity Red'**
see p. 264

Ⓒ **Lobelia 'Sapphire'**
see p. 128

A (above)

Designing with Cannas

Canna lilies are tremendously versatile and work equally well in flower beds and containers. They are also easy to overwinter and get larger every year, which makes enjoying their massive foliage surprisingly affordable. If you can't find them in the annuals section of your favourite garden centre, look for them with the water plants; cannas are marginals and can easily be grown in the water (photo B).

In the past few years, cannas have been most sought after for container plants. They bring an instant sense of jungle to designs; their massive leaves have a sense of being untamed as they pour oxygen and humidity

B (above); C (below)

into the garden. I found the container in photo A on a patio at Earl's. The leaves create an impression of a wall, which effectively splits up the patio.

In Quebec City we saw cannas being used in a bed to soften a wall. The rich red leaves harmonize with the soft pink gaura, which is used as a filler row against the massive backdrop of leaves (photo C).

Mountain of Pink

Height: to 1 m · **Spread:** to 1 m

WHEN IT COMES to colour, sometimes bigger is better! The Vista Series of trailing petunias packs the most colour of any other annual I've encountered. Put it in a very simple recipe like this one, and you have a blast of pure, joyful colour that's perfect for pulling the eye into the far corners of your garden. Even from a distance, the petunias are such a vivacious pink that the colour will pop.

A Purple fountain grass

B Petunia 'Supertunia Vista Bubblegum'

C Petunia 'Supertunia Vista Fuchsia'

Petunia 'Supertunia Vista Silverberry'

Recommended container size:
45–70 cm across

Remember the good ol' days when the only petunias available were in a six-pack and you cheered if you got a flower out of them by June? While the recent explosion in varieties of trailing petunias has certainly made the shopping experience more complicated, it has also made it exponentially more rewarding.

Here's a hint: when you're shopping for petunias, check the tag for the size of each one. Some new types, like the Potunia Series, look gorgeous on the bench because they are the first to bloom but don't get very large in the garden. Other types, like the Vista Series, may not look be impressive on the bench but turn into garden giants!

The sheer size of Vistas can be a bit overwhelming, so the wispy fountain grass is important to soften the look. Besides adding an airy verticality to the otherwise plain bell shape, pulling our eyes upward so our gaze doesn't settle in the mass of pink flowers and get trapped there, its feathered plumes bring a light-hearted whimsy. As they catch the breeze, the movement will catch your eye, even from a distance.

Because of its complete lack of subtlety, I would put this container a fair distance from where I like to sit and relax. Differently scaled containers and flower beds can play with perspective in the garden. If you put a recipe using smaller, more diminutive ingredients far away from you, it will make the distance seem even farther. A design like this one, with unusually large plants, will condense the space between subject and object, making the garden appear to be a smaller space than it actually is.

'Vista' Supertunias make outstanding hanging baskets; just make sure that you fertilize them as much as you can and keep them well watered.

Ⓐ Purple fountain grass
Pennisetum setaceum

Although this container doesn't emphasize texture or vertical appeal, without the fountain grass it would just look like a mass of colour. The sun-loving grass rescues it from shapelessness by adding something other than colour to entertain the eye. The way the feathery plumes catch the wind is wonderful to watch.

Ⓑ Ⓒ Petunia 'Supertunia Vista' Series
Petunia x *hybrida;* trailing petunia

There are several colours of Vista petunias available, including 'Vista Bubblegum,' 'Vista Fuchsia' and 'Vista Silverberry.' I find that 'Vista Bubblegum' is the best combination of yummy colour and controllable (relatively speaking) growth habit. 'Vista Fuchsia,' being the original, is the darkest pink and tends to be the most out of control. As with all trailing petunias, Vistas love lots of sun and copious amounts of fertilizer.

Using Trailing Petunias

Vista petunias are fairly easy to find, affordable (compared to other big annuals) and easy to care for once they're established. They are very versatile; if you have a spot where you want big colour and you're not especially concerned about the subtleties of design, then throw a few Vistas in and watch the colour explode. They would be perfect on the periphery of the garden where you need a mass impact that draws the eye from a long way off.

You can get creative with trailing petunias as well. On the Proven Winners website is an intriguing three-tiered planter that, if you can keep it watered, would be a guaranteed conversation starter (photo A).

A (bottom left); B (above)

Trailing petunias love hanging baskets—a little too much, actually. If the basket isn't large enough, it will dry out very quickly as the plant grows (and grows and grows). Petunias aren't drought tolerant, so a dry basket can be bad news during a drought. The ground is often too cold for their tropical root systems, but a raised bed or planter is the perfect compromise. Mix them with pink gaura and bacopa for a high-impact bed that will bloom all summer in full sun (photo B).

Height: 1 m • **Spread:** to 1 m

THIS DESIGN IS A GREAT example of how a powerful centrepiece can frame and define everything around it. It's a recipe that uses densely packed colour and foliage to create a potent tropical look. All the ingredients are punctuated by a massive dracaena spike in the centre, its long leaves piercing everything around it. You can plant it in a window box, but if you want to be able to see out the window, you should keep the box on the ground.

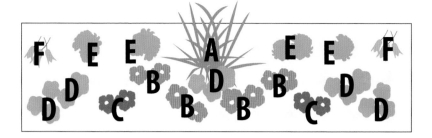

A Dracaena spike

B Petunia 'Potunia Neon'

C Petunia 'Potunia Red'

D Calibrachoa 'Superbells Apricot Punch'

E Geranium 'Indian Dunes'

F Begonia 'Million Kisses'

Recommended container size:
35 cm by 75 cm

This recipe would look stunning as the centrepiece to a tropical-themed part of your garden, surrounded by other lush foliage and ferns. The colours create a tropical frenzy of warm, summer sun colours, and the vivacious leaves blend together to create a dramatic showpiece.

A specimen dracaena spike dominates this composition. The other plants grow up and around it, weaving between the long leaves that pierce their way outward. Dracaenas and cordylines work well in containers because if you draw a line connecting the tips of their leaves, then take the plant away, you'll be left with a pleasing egg shape. Here, the dracaena's outline invites the eye to travel in radial directions around the composition, like a guide helping you to explore it.

To grow a dracaena into a large specimen, you will need to overwinter it inside for a few years. It's an attractive enough houseplant and likes a sunny window. If you have very small children, be careful because the tips of the leaves are sharp.

This fuchsia standard from Rideau Hall is an excellent example of how you can grow a plant to an impressive size by brining it indoors over winter.

Ⓐ Dracaena spike

Dracaena indivisa; spike

The common dracaena, like the red geranium, has gotten a reputation as a boring plant as a result of decades of overuse. It is far from boring and still has a lot to offer modern designers and the innovative containers they're putting together. Dracaenas love full sun and can handle a lot of heat, and they are drought tolerant, though often their container-mates aren't.

Ⓑ Petunia 'Potunia Neon' and
Ⓒ 'Potunia Red'

Petunia x *hybrida;* trailing petunia

Potunias are quite new to the market but have already made a big splash. They stay more compact than Supertunias, so while they won't fill out a massive container as quickly, they tend to burst into bloom sooner. They're perfect when you want a lot of colour in a small to medium container, and they keep a pleasing, upright shape longer than other petunias.

Ⓓ Calibrachoa 'Superbells Apricot Punch'
see p. 124

Ⓔ Geranium 'Indian Dunes'
see p. 220

Ⓕ Begonia 'Million Kisses'
see p. 116

Growing Specimen Ingredients

If you're keen on designing and creating impressive container gardens, I strongly recommend that you devote a section of your den or bedroom near a sunny window to overwintering specimen plants. Every year you keep a dracaena, cordyline, phormium, alocasia or a host of other centrepiece plants, they will be larger and more impressive the next spring and will add an instant maturity to your garden, even in May. Overwintering bulbs of canna lilies and colocasia will be reap the same rewards.

One of the wonderful things about keeping dracaena and cordyline as multi-year plants is the gorgeous

A (above); B (below)

egg-like shape they take on when they are mature. The filler plants grow up and in between the thick leaves (or blades), creating the illusion that the fillers are being skewered (photo A).

The container with the 'Red Sensation' cordyline was planted with a multi-year specimen (photo B). If the designer had used a smaller plant (even a very expensive store-bought cordyline wouldn't be as large), the container would have had a completely different look.

Bellini

Height: to 70 cm • **Spread:** to 60 cm

IT'S A GOOD IDEA to build a design around one thematic element. Here, I take it one step further, using the other plants as a frame around my thematic element so that wherever you look, your eye goes right to the gazania. While the warm colours compete for space as fillers, the harmonizing cool colours and vertical shapes of the phormium and lysimachia (one grows straight up and the other straight down) frame the scene and direct the eye to the focal point in the centre.

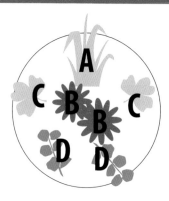

A Phormium 'Yellow Wave'

B Gazania 'Sunbathers'

C Oxalis 'Molten Lava'

D Lysimachia 'Goldilocks'

Recommended container size:
40–55 cm across

This recipe is a delicious blend of warm Mediterranean tones and cool, trendy greens and limes. There are a lot of subtle textures and colours at play here, from the red stems of the oxalis to the electric green lines of the phormium. I built this container to highlight the gazania, which is nestled in front of a backdrop of phormium and in between some fast-growing oxalis, and whether your eye is climbing the lysimachia or looking between the oxalis, everything brings you back to the gazania.

Keep this container in a hot, exposed spot. While gazania is stunning when it's sunbathing, like all sun-worshippers it closes its flowers and pouts under cloudy skies. You may have to step in occasionally to protect it, as it's nestled between two very aggressive oxalis plants.

If you don't like the idea of your thematic element closing up and pouting on cloudy days, you can easily substitute it with another warm-coloured filler such as 'Superbells Tequila Sunrise' calibrachoa. Or, you could use a cool-coloured annual, like a 'Supertunia Citrus' petunia, and change the dominant colour scheme of the design.

This container vividly showcases the radically different textures of oxalis and phormium, providing excitement for the viewer as they clash against each other.

ⓐ Phormium 'Yellow Wave'

Phormium tenax; New Zealand flax

When it comes to grasses, you don't have to be dark red to be beautiful! Blonde phormiums bring a cool sense of modernity to recipes and can always be brought inside in fall. Keep it year after year to create a magnificent specimen.

ⓑ Gazania 'Sunbathers'

Gazania rigens; treasure flower

New to the market, 'Sunbathers' is a double-flowering gazania that, while gorgeous, isn't quite as free-blooming as the Kiss Series. If I did this container again, I would trade the double flowers of 'Sunbathers' for more numerous, yellow flowers of 'Big Kiss' gazania.

ⓒ Oxalis 'Molten Lava'

Oxalis vulcanicola; false shamrock

This oxalis hit the gardening world about the same time as the darker-leafed and better-known Charmed Series. 'Molten Lava' has smaller leaves, the stems are a rich red and it has a voracious growth habit that will send you running for the rescue scissors. It's easy to grow and boasts gorgeous colours but might be hard to find, so call some garden centres before you head out.

ⓓ Lysimachia 'Goldilocks'

see p. 196

Using Phormium in Designs

The more you know about the growth habits of different plants, the more you can use them to your advantage in containers. I find that phormium and oxalis pair beautifully with each other because their habits are so radically different that they just seem to work together. While phormium is tidy, clean-cut and architecturally alluring, oxalis is messy and voracious, spreading in as many directions as it can, as quickly as it can, and gobbling up whatever other plants it can along the way.

When combined with the messiness of oxalis, which will even be cheeky enough to creep between the phormium blades, phormium

A (above); B (below)

creates a sharp and playful contrast of competing habits and shapes (photo A).

Phormium tends to grow into a fan shape, unlike dracaena and cordyline, which grow into a bell shape. When used effectively, phormium can act as a backdrop of dramatically straight lines to highlight the plants in front of it (photo B).

Pink Explosion

Height: to 1 m • **Spread:** to 70 cm

IF YOU DON'T like pink, this recipe isn't for you. I call this one "Pink Explosion" because it's full of movement and vitality. There is a palpable sense of energy in the multiple shades of pink that makes it seem to dance, especially when the sunlight plays between the different textures. From the airy gaura vaulting into the sky to the bulky geraniums clustered below like boulders, this container tells a vivid story.

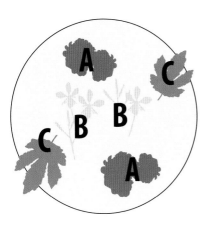

Ⓐ Zonal geranium

Ⓑ Gaura 'Stratosphere Pink Picotee'

Ⓓ Hibiscus 'Red Shield'

Recommended container size:
40–55 cm across

This design is living proof that an analogous colour scheme can be as vibrant and dynamic as a complementary one. The different pinks here, from the soft gaura to the bold, stabilizing hibiscus, provide enough textural contrast and playful movement to fascinate the eye and keep it coming back for more.

Use this container as a focal point in full sun. If you plant according to the diagram, you'll be able to enjoy it from all sides, making it perfect for the middle of a deck or just in the centre of the yard, possibly with smaller, harmonious pots around it. If you only want to see if from one side, adjust the design to have the larger hibiscus and guara in the back. If you put it in a taller container, you might want to add some pink calibrachoa around the base to provide some trailing appeal.

'Red Shield' hibiscus makes a rich harmony with red Supertunias.

Ⓐ Zonal geranium

Pelargonium x *hortorum*

Yes, it's still okay to use geraniums! In the past 30 years they have been so overused that they have become synonymous with an old-fashioned style of gardening. It's a label I consider unfair because they are gorgeous annuals, and new varieties are constantly improving them. You will need to deadhead them once the flower clusters are spent.

Ⓑ Gaura 'Stratosphere Pink Picotee'

Gaura lindheimeri; butterfly flower

As usual, the gaura is what really brings this recipe to life! Whether it's the way it arcs upward or how the delicate flowers catch every breeze, it makes the container move; gaura is the ingredient that really tells the story. Make sure it's in full sun, and don't be afraid to nip off old shoots once they are finished blooming.

Ⓓ Hibiscus 'Red Shield'

Hibiscus acetosella; 'Coppertone'

With beautifully crafted, oak-shaped leaves and a delicious deep red colour, this is an exciting and surprisingly versatile foliage stuffer. It grows quickly in the heat and in mid to late summer blooms small, dark pink, mallow flowers. Make sure you buy one with several branches, or all you will get is a very pretty stick.

Gaura: Perfect for Designing

For both design potential and raw visual appeal, gaura is one the best annuals out there to include in your compositions. It blooms sequentially up the flower spike, so it stays in bloom for the entire summer. The pink gaura has undertones of various shades of pink, making it ideal for harmonizing with darker pink and even rich purple plants (photo A).

Like a flock of flamingos filling the sky as they vault into the air, gaura

A (bottom left); B (above)

pulses with energy and adds a sense of vibrant ascension to any design it's in. Add gaura to a design with low-growing, heavy-blooming performers such as trailing petunias and bacopa to give the container an uplifting sense of buoyancy (photo B).

The thing about gaura that makes it so useful in designs is that it plays with us. Our eyes see it and want to explore the cloud of fluttering butterflies, trying to see if all of them are really connected. While the white gaura has an innocent, almost childlike playfulness to it, the pink is more versatile in its moods and will range from pure joy in mid-day to a slightly more sombre presence at twilight as its darker tones absorb the diminishing light.

The Crooked Grin

Height: to 1.2 m • **Spread:** to 60 cm

WHEN IT COMES to your garden, you make the rules. Your design doesn't have to be pretty to be breathtaking. I made this design because I wanted to create a container that reminded people of a smile on a comic book super-villain: twisted and a little sinister, but mesmerizing. Starting with the double datura as my thematic element, I chose ingredients with deeply serrated lines, brooding colours and jagged angles. The result is a recipe that excites the deep corners of my imagination.

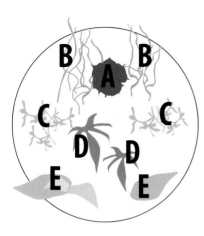

Ⓐ Datura 'Ballerina Purple'

Ⓑ Curly willow

Ⓒ Euphorbia 'Diamond Frost'

Ⓓ Sweet potato vine 'Illusion Midnight Lace'

Ⓔ Zebrina tradescantia

Recommended container size:
35–45 cm across

In live theatre, purple is considered one of the best colours to use because it's so versatile, its moods ranging from sinister and brooding in low light to energetic and alive in high light. The purple here will behave the same way, so watch it in different light conditions and enjoy!

This recipe would be perfect in a grouping of other purple, modern designs. Feel free to substitute freely, especially with the poisonous datura if you have small children or nibbly pets. The 'Diamond Frost' euphorbia and the sweet potato vine will blend well together no matter what the centrepiece is.

Put this container in a sunny spot, possibly with some protection from the late afternoon sun, and keep it well watered. Generous amounts of fertilizer will keep its shape compact and the colours rich.

'Superbells Blackberry Punch' is perfect for creating designs with a dark side. It looks sinister and will bloom profusely all summer.

Ⓐ Datura 'Ballerina Purple'
Datura metel; angel's trumpet

I wanted to showcase this exquisitely fiendish plant. Its jagged leaves and rich purple blooms make it the perfect villain of the garden. Pinch the spiky seed pods when they form to keep it blooming longer, but make sure to either wear gloves or wash your hands whenever you touch it.

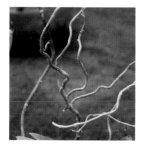

Ⓑ Curly willow
Salix matsudana

The willow has the last word on the crooked shape of the design. There are many branches available in larger garden centres that industrious gardeners can use to bring instant verticality and a heightened sense of modernity to their designs. You may have to buy curly willow at Christmas because it's often hard to find in spring. If you put it in water, it will sprout up and down the stems.

Ⓒ Euphorbia 'Diamond Frost'
see p. 148

Ⓓ Sweet potato vine 'Illusion Midnight Lace'
Ipomoea batatas

The Illusion Series of sweet potato vines boasts startling, deeply serrated leaves that blend perfectly in contemporary containers where shape and clean lines are the priority. It has the same beefy growth habit as other sweet potato vines and is maintenance free in full sun or partial shade.

Ⓔ Zebrina tradescantia
Tradescantia zebrina; inch plant, wandering Jew

Tradescantia is a common vine indoors that savvy gardeners are starting to use on the patio. Its variegated leaves add visual appeal, but you will need to protect it from the sweet potato vine, at least until it gets established. Watch for signs of burning if it's exposed to the afternoon scorch.

Designs with a Dark Side

I had a great time designing the feature ("The Crooked Grin") because I love making containers with personality, and making a container with a dark side was an exciting challenge. Even though this style isn't for everybody,

A (above); B (below)

there are plenty of options out there if you want to design your own twisted composition. Look for dark colours, jagged textures and twisting, contorted shapes.

The Illusion Series of sweet potato vines is ideal for building designs that are up to no good. Its heavily serrated leaves provide a perfectly jagged look (photo B).

If you want to create a design with a dark side, but perhaps not quite as sinister as the feature, consider softening it with some fountain grass or millet. The more straight, jagged lines you replace with curving,

rounded lines, the less sinister it becomes, allowing you to find the ideal balance between making a container with attitude and one that's downright scary (photo A).

Slow-Motion Explosion

Height: to 2 m • **Spread:** to 70 cm

MY WIFE HAS a flawless eye for design, and as I watched her choose the ingredients for this recipe, I knew it would be gorgeous. The contrasting shades and shapes dancing together, from the tiny talinum flowers to the trumpeting mandevilla to the long, sleek fountain grass, explode with a gentle ease that is energizing to look at.

A Mandevilla 'Sun Parasol Pink'

B Talinum 'Limon'

C Calibrachoa 'Superbells
Tickled Pink'

D Purple fountain grass 'Fireworks'

Recommended container size:
40–50 cm across

Flowering vines can make stunning centrepieces because they often have more body to them than more conventional "thrillers." You may have to rescue the filler plants from eager lower tendrils. This recipe would make an excellent centrepiece for a grouping of other, simpler mixes using some of the same ingredients.

It's versatile, too. In the photo I've used it to frame a doorway. It would also thrive against a south- or west-facing wall on the deck, where it can be delightfully grown against light-coloured siding. If you install a trellis on the wall, the mandevilla will climb it for even more impact—just don't expect it to grow 3 metres in a season like it does in Hawaii.

You can keep mandevilla year after year, but make sure to clean it very well in fall in case it has picked up critters, and be warned that it often looks downright ugly in winter.

'Superbells Strawberry Punch' is a playful blend of pinks that will provide instant harmony to any pink-themed colour scheme.

A Mandevilla 'Sun Parasol Pink'

Mandevilla sanderi; dipladenia

I had gotten so used to the 'Alice du Pont' mandevilla, with its characteristic big leaves and massive pink flowers, that I was reluctant to try the new Parasol Series. Once I saw it in action, I was a convert! Although the flowers are smaller than the older varieties, it blooms like crazy in the summer heat while still retaining the tropical lipstick pink that made us fall in love with mandevilla in the first place.

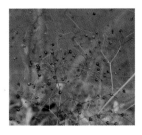

B Talinum 'Limon'

Talinum paniculatum; jewels of Opar

One of my favourite introductions from the past few years, talinum starts the season with striking lime foliage, then in the early summer shoots long panicles of tiny, white, floating flowers into the air that harden into caramel seed pods in July. Make sure it's not exposed to temperatures below about 4° Celsius.

C Calibrachoa 'Superbells Tickled Pink'

see p. 124

D Purple fountain grass 'Fireworks'

Pennisetum setaceum; red fountain grass

A welcome change from the ubiquitous burgundies of grasses, 'Fireworks' is a rich reddish pink that keeps its colour with some warm sun and generous amounts of fertilizer. It stays compact enough to be used as a filler.

Designing for Movement

One of the things that really makes the feature ("Slow-Motion Explosion") work is the that many elements are reaching outward in all directions, giving the illusion of an explosion frozen in time. A very low-growing, dense annual, like an upright petunia, looks motionless in a container because it's not reaching outward, whereas airy plants such as talinum,

A (bottom left); B (above)

euphorbia and gaura seem like they are in motion because they are constantly reaching outward as if trying to break free of their container.

Heuchera illustrates how dramatically a sense of movement can change the feel of a design. It is a compact foliage perennial that explodes in summer. The sparse flowers bloom along vertical spikes that reach outward in all directions. When they bloom, they change the design of the container as completely as the heuchera changes from a compact, motionless plant to being full of movement and excitement as it vaults out of its confines (photo B).

Spooned osteospermums capture a sense of movement in a more subtle way. Their alien-like flowers are like fireworks crackling with life as they burst into tiny explosions in the container (photo A). If you want your design to capture a sense of movement but keep a sense of elegance and shape, then these unique plants may be perfect for you.

Height: to 2 m • **Spread:** to 60 cm

THERE ARE A LOT of traditional ways to celebrate the colour yellow in the garden—think sunflowers and yellow pansies—but I wanted to design a yellow container that had a modern flair to it and that emphasized shape as well as colour. When I found some Swiss chard growing in vegetable tubs in the back greenhouses, I knew I had my design. The colours in this container are pure, honest and bursting with excitement. Unorthodox shapes will keep the eye eager to explore, but I predict that your gaze will always come back to the contrasting, elegantly symmetrical Swiss chard leaves.

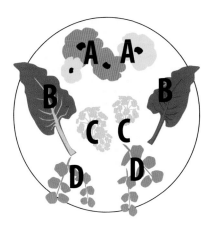

🅐 Thunbergia 'Sunny'

🅑 Swiss chard 'Bright Lights'

🅒 Lantana 'Luscious Lemonade'

🅓 Lysimachia 'Goldilocks'

Recommended container size:
  40–55 cm across

Swiss chard is yet another example of taking a plant out of its ordinary role and using it to make something extraordinary. I remember seeing it in containers and beds in Paris and marvelling how the vibrant, pure colour of the stems glowed through the circulatory system of the leaves. It tastes great too, of course; I like it with a light boil and some butter. If you plan to eat it, harvest the occasional leaf from around the plant so it doesn't get lopsided.

This container will make a great focal point in full sun; it will even thrive on your hot deck where the black-eyed Susan vine can climb high on a trellis. I used curly willow to add a more dynamic shape. The trellis you use goes a long way in determining the overall shape of the container. As the summer rolls on, the lantana will start to bloom like crazy; it needs the heat to thrive.

'Goldilocks' lysimachia hangs straight down from a container, bringing a sense of vertical line even as a trailer.

🅐 Thunbergia 'Sunny'
Thunbergia alata; black-eyed Susan vine

Although released only a few years ago, 'Sunny' has quickly become one of the most popular flowering vines around. The flowers are some of the purest, warmest colours available, each one sharply contrasting with its black-eyed centre. Make sure it's in full sun and gets ample fertilizer for its fast-paced growth habit.

🅑 Swiss chard 'Bright Lights'
Beta vulgaris

If you haven't tried Swiss chard in a garden design yet, you should try it this spring. The stems are warm colours so pure they almost glow, and the plant requires almost no maintenance. You may want to remove the older leaves that droop low because they will cover up the bright colours and crowd other stuffers planted around them.

🅒 Lantana 'Luscious Lemonade'
see p. 244

🅓 Lysimachia 'Goldilocks'
Lysimachia nummularia; creeping Jenny

This terrifically versatile vine grows like crazy in full sun. Although it will grow several feet long in a season, it takes up very little volume inside the container, making it a great choice for giving small containers the illusion of being larger.

Using Lime Green

Lime green has become a very trendy colour scheme in the past few years. Vivacious and full of life, lime green is great for designing because it has the potential to provide vibrant contrast with anything blue or purple. The sassy colour also tends to reflect the sun, so on a bright day a lime green container can appear to glow, making for a vivid Mediterranean warmth that can light up the whole garden.

One obstacle to designing with lime green is that it clashes with more colours than some other colour schemes. I recommend sticking to either a direct contrasting design (i.e., mixed with purple flowers) or a harmonious design that hugs a few

A (above); B (below)

bars on the colour wheel, as in photo A and the feature ("Mediterranean Sunrise").

Lime green is ideal for monochromatic containers, and because it's so popular, there are new ingredients coming out all the time that you can use. Bright yellow will work in the design if you try to balance it with some slightly greener tones (photo B).

Before Sunrise

Height: to 1 m • **Spread:** to 60 cm

LOOKING AT THIS container, you would never guess that its two main ingredients are houseplants, which are often overlooked for designs. The sublimely dark leaves, glistening as if they had just been through a jungle rain, reach out in every direction to create a thick sense of canopy while vines and flowers prosper on the sheltered forest floor. A sleek, rich colour palette and a flurry of textural contrasts combine to make a striking recipe.

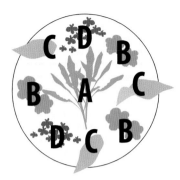

Ⓐ Cordyline 'Black Magic'

Ⓑ Begonia 'Illumination Apricot'

Ⓒ Zebrina tradescantia

Ⓓ Lobelia 'Laguna Heavenly Lilac'

Recommended container size:
35–45 cm across

The centrepiece plant is a 'Black Magic' cordyline, a fairly common houseplant grown in Florida and often available at larger garden centres. If you don't fancy the dark leaves, there are other varieties available, including the striking burgundy-red 'Red Sister.'

The flowers underneath are an eye-catching dance of harmony and contrast. The tradescantia links the eye to the cordyline, visually condensing the container vertically, while the begonia adds a well-placed splash of contrast that is playful but not glaring. If you wanted to add more contrast, you could stuff some variegated spider plants into the mix.

This container would bring a rich lushness to a sheltered patio. I would combine it with other tropical elements in lilac, purple or yellow, perhaps in smaller, simpler recipes with this one as the centrepiece. It would also look great in a shady nook somewhere, possibly by a water feature with other tropical elements or a hosta bed.

With its intense hot pink leaves, 'Red Sister' cordyline is ideal for zesty designs in sheltered spots.

🅐 Cordyline 'Black Magic'

Cordyline fruticosa; cabbage palm

Cordyline will thrive outside, protected from the afternoon sun, in humid regions. If you live in a drier region, like the Prairies, a water feature will help. A daily blast with the hose will keep it moist and help keep spider mites off its leaves, which it tends to attract, especially in hot, dry weather.

🅑 Begonia 'Illumination Apricot'

Begonia x *hybrida;* trailing begonia

The Illumination Series is a reliable workhorse that will keep flowering all summer as long as you keep up on fertilizing and watering. Make sure it's protected from the afternoon sun.

🅒 Zebrina tradescantia

Tradescantia zebrina; inch plant, wandering Jew

This playful vine boasts uniquely variegated foliage and a lot of versatility; it seems able to slink its way into almost any recipe and look good doing it. It can be trained to tolerate afternoon sun, but it won't like it.

🅓 Lobelia 'Laguna Heavenly Lilac'

see p. 284

Dark Leaves in Design

I'm a sucker for dark-leafed plants in container design. The feature container ("Before Sunrise") caught my eye both because it boasts dark, glistening leaves and because the central ingredient is a houseplant not normally used in outdoor container design.

People who like using dark leaves usually love contrast. Almost everything contrasts with black in some way. If you throw some bright red flowers into the mix, the design will take on an almost sinister tone, with red flowers and the green and black leaves all clashing against each other (photo A).

If you want to have high contrast that leans toward a contemporary style, then try the brash contrast of white on black. You can find this mix in one plant, like 'Charmed Velvet' oxalis (photo B), or by combining several white and black elements to create a powerful look.

A (above), B (below)

White and black containers are usually very modern, often using rigid, distinct lines, but they can also be cold and unfeeling and are an acquired taste. From a design point of view, they are the opposite of the cottage style, which stresses warmth and relaxation.

Blue Bouquet

Height: to 50 cm • **Spread:** to 60 cm

BLUE IS AN ENIGMATIC, fascinating colour. It has so many moods; it can be vivacious and carefree as it blooms in the sunlight, or dark, brooding and mysterious. It's the colour of the sky, and we're so familiar with it that no matter its mood, blue is always somehow soothing to look at. This design explores the different moods of blue, and, by offsetting it with sparking white petunias, the blue is allowed to breathe and become its optimistic best.

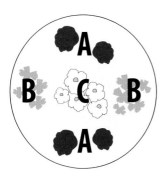

A Torenia 'Summer Wave Blue'

B Verbena 'Babylon Light Blue'

C Petunia 'Supertunia White'

Recommended container size:
    35–45 cm across

Both elegant and cheerful, this design manages to exude an air of poise without being pretentious and inspire smiles without being goofy. It has a universal quality and will still be popular once the current trends have moved on and some of the other recipes in this book become passé.

Much of the charm of this container is in its compact, curving outline. If you want to keep it like that, you will need to do some occasional pinching, especially on the petunias. The torenia and verbena will stay slightly more compact, though they are both still likely to need some maintenance.

Notice how elegant the pot is here. This recipe would lose some of its appeal if it were planted in a basic plastic pot. Look through your pots for something that fits the style or, if you do use a plain pot, I recommend allowing the plants to trail over or adding a trailer such as lobelia.

You're going to want to keep this container close to you. It would fit perfectly into a sunny sitting area with other blues. If you want to create a contemporary feel, try blending it with smaller containers of echeveria succulents (the rosette succulents with blue hues to them).

Keep it in full sun and make sure the soil doesn't dry out too much. Generous amounts of fertilizer will keep the foliage a rich green. As I mentioned above, keep the scissors handy if you want to preserve its compact shape.

Blue and white blend beautifully together, leaving you free to experiment with textures and shapes knowing that the colour scheme will work.

Ⓐ Torenia 'Summer Wave Blue'
Torenia fournieri; wishbone flower

The original series of trailing torenia, 'Summer Wave' performs beautifully, producing scores of blue-throated trumpets in mid-summer. It may even attract hummingbirds.

Ⓑ Verbena 'Babylon Light Blue'
Verbena x hybrida; trailing verbena

This light shade of blue is the middle colour between the white and dark blue of the design, and it's what gives the design its fluidity. Watch for powdery mildew if it's in a spot with poor air movement or in periods of cool, cloudy weather.

Ⓒ Petunia 'Supertunia White'
see p. 112

Designing with Blue

Blue and white is a great combination for an elegant, soothing container; purple and pink is a slightly zestier combo that can be just as elegant while providing a little more exuberance. Purple and pink are harmonious colours, so any design using them will still have a soothing quality, and within that mix you can use lavenders and lilacs as well (photo A).

The Artist Series of ageratum is perfect for a purple/pink colour scheme

A (below)

B (above); C (below)

because it has both (photo B)! It stays nicely compact but doesn't like hot weather much and may wilt in the July scorch. It will look amazing in spring, though, and pairs nicely with 'Soprano' osteospermum, blue bacopa or 'Intensia' phlox.

For small containers, 'Soprano' osteospermums are excellent. The plants are compact, bloom like crazy and don't tend to get as leggy as their yellow and orange 'Symphony' cousins. A small pot with some purple 'Soprano' osteos and some euphorbia would fit perfectly into a sunny sitting space (photo C).

Silver Cascades

Height: to 1 m • **Spread:** to 60 cm

WE PLANTED A NUMBER of pots of this recipe, and they always caught my eye when I walked past them in the greenhouse. Their dense yet exuberant sense of movement reminded me of a slow-motion storm, each element swirling around the other in a mass of delicate shapes and textures. Each one was a celebration of small, vibrant ingredients and how they can all work together.

Ⓐ Dracaena spike

Ⓑ Euphorbia 'Diamond Frost'

Calibrachoa 'Superbells Cherry Blossom'

Ⓓ Dichondra 'Silver Falls'

Recommended container size:
35–45 cm across

Everything is in motion here. Tiny leaves and flowers layer over each other, all working and flowing together to create a harmonious whole that pulses with movement. In container design, large central flowers, like dahlias and petunias, do more than bring a lot of colour. They often act as an anchor, stabilizing the design like a foot holding down a kite on a windy day. In this recipe, though there are very few contrasting colours at play, the lack of a large stabilizing element makes it pulse with movement.

Because there is such a sense of movement, I would pair this container with much simpler recipes that use the same plants. Some containers around it with pink calibrachoa, euphorbia or just a dracaena spike will accent the container while providing some calming simplicity.

Anywhere this container goes, it's going to bring a unique combination

of movement and elegance. Its cool colour palette and flurry of textures would make it an exciting addition to a patio or to a garden with similar themes. It will need to be in a sunny spot, but all the elements are slightly drought tolerant. Use a metallic (either real or synthetic) container to heighten the effect.

You can substitute any colour of calibrachoa in this design. A darker colour will visually ground it, while lighter colours are more playful.

Ⓐ Dracaena spike

Dracaena indivisa; spike

Although they've been overused in the past, dracaenas are still one of the most reliable and easy-to-care-for centrepieces available. The shape of their long leaves brings a nostalgic sense of architecture to any container or flower bed they're in.

Ⓑ Euphorbia 'Diamond Frost'

Euphorbia hybrid; diamond frost

Euphorbia provides much of the storm effect, with its crisp, white blooms clustering into dense clouds. Keep it on the dry side in the hot sun. Euphorbia provides a dynamic contrast of shape with the long, clean lines of dracaena.

Calibrachoa 'Superbells Cherry Blossom'

see p. 124

Ⓓ Dichondra 'Silver Falls'

Dichondra argentea; kidney weed

Although fairly new to the market, dichondra is already popular thanks to its kidney-shaped, soft silver leaves that layer straight downward like a suit of mail armour. It grows quickly with very little maintenance.

Creating Elegance

Elegance can be an elusive quality to capture in a container. As the feature design ("Silver Cascades") illustrates, elegance need not necessarily mean compactness. A container can have a sense of poise and dignity without being compact and perfectly mani-cured. If you're looking to achieve a sense of elegance in your designs, the first thing I recommend is to stick with a cool colour palette. Silvers, soft blues and crisp greens are all ideal.

Make sure the actual container fits the atmosphere you're trying to create.

Elegance can come from a sense of balance in the container. When no one ingredient towers over the others, there is often a subtle sense of restraint and tension. Photo A features hostas, blush-coloured 'Non-Stop' begonias and bacopa. Set in a classical urn and with an angel bust in the centre, the balance

A (above); B (below)

between the begonias and the hostas brings a sense of poise with it.

Single plants can be elegant as well. We planted a container of laurentia outside Salisbury, and I was surprised at how great it looked on its own (photo B). Its soft colour and delicate, almost lace-like leaves make it a gorgeous plant that can add a dose of low-maintenance elegance to a garden.

Summer Elegance

Height: to 40 cm · **Spread:** to 90 cm

VIVID, BRIGHT COLOURS are beautiful, but a whole garden full of them can be exhausting. Our eyes can rest on a softer, more soothing colour scheme, one that relaxes rather than invigorates. This combination uses the softer side of the blue palette to create a harmonic container perfect for a garden nook where you can go to clear your head. Its bell shape and lack of starkly contrasting shapes reinforce its calming effect.

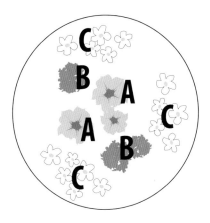

Ⓐ Petunia 'Supertunia Mini Blue Veined'

Ⓑ Verbena 'Superbena Dark Blue'

Ⓒ Bacopa 'Snowstorm'

Recommended container size:
35–50 cm across

I would use this container as one element in a relaxing sitting area. Blue is such a versatile colour that there's a lot you can do with it. If you want to create a relaxing sitting area, use this container as a guide and head to the garden centre to choose other plants with harmonious colours and shapes. You can use a variety of containers (hanging baskets, patio pots, small tabletop pots) filled with soft blue tones to create a perfectly relaxing, almost nautical-themed, garden nook to sit in.

If you want to keep it as compactly shaped as it is in the picture, frequent pinching back will be required. The petunias especially will try to outgrow the verbena and the bacopa, so don't be shy about clipping them back as long as you fertilize regularly. If you aren't concerned about keeping the compact bell shape, then put the pruners away and enjoy as it pours over the sides of the pot.

This container will need full sun. During wet, cool, overcast periods the ingredients will start to get leggy and pale; pinch them and they will bounce back.

Petunias and million bells are a perfect example of harmonious shapes that blend well together.

Ⓐ Petunia 'Supertunia Mini Blue Veined'
Petunia x *hybrida;* trailing petunia

Although it's not as flashy as some of the other Supertunia colours, 'Mini Blue Veined' has an impressive growth habit and blooms profusely in the sun all summer. It's recognizable by its blue throat, which gets darker as the throat curves inward.

Ⓑ Verbena 'Superbena Dark Blue'
Verbena x *hybrida;* trailing verbena

Verbena looks as good in relaxing colours as it does in invigorating ones. As long as it has sun and fertilizer, it's an effortless plant to grow. It's more drought resistant than petunias, but that doesn't matter as much in this container; with the bacopa around you'll need to keep it consistently moist.

Ⓒ Bacopa 'Snowstorm'
Sutera cordata; water hyssop

The small bacopa flowers balance out the larger petunias and add a hint of contrast. If you want to be consistent with the blues, use 'Snowstorm Blue,' which has almost as pleasing a growth habit as the white.

Compact Designs

When it comes to making compact containers with a perfect bell shape to them, putting them together is usually the easy part. In May when all the plants in the garden centre are looking their best, some people think that they will just stay that size and keep blooming away happily. They don't, of course, and with compact designs especially, it's important to keep growth habits in mind when planting.

You can still use high-performance annuals such as trailing petunias in your compact designs, but you need

A (bottom left); B (above)

to recognize that after a month or so you will have to either intervene with your scissors or let the shape of the container change. Keeping a perfect bell shape takes a little extra effort, but for some gardeners it's well worth it (photo A).

Euphorbia is a great accent to a compact container. It doesn't tend to grow very large on its own, and even when it does it responds well to trimming. It exists to complement the showier plants in the design, like a side-kick in an old western movie. In photo B, 'Tukana Deep Red' verbena is made even more spectacular thanks to its container-mate.

Parade

Height: to 50 cm · **Spread:** to 80 cm

PEOPLE WHO DON'T love colour need not apply! This container is a celebration of colour, from a delicious, juicy orange to a stark, dramatic red. Many contemporary trends are focused on using foliage plants in containers, and it's easy to forget that a composition can be striking, trendy *and* colourful if we use the right ingredients. Here, the juncus adds enough stark architecture to make it contemporary while the other plants pour out enough colour to make it unforgettable.

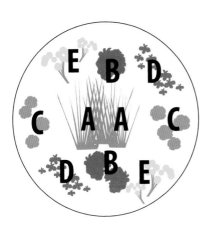

Ⓐ Juncus 'Javelin'

Ⓑ Zonal geranium

Ⓒ Calibrachoa 'Superbells Dreamsicle'

Ⓓ Lobelia 'Laguna Sky Blue'

Ⓔ Chrysocephalum 'Flambe'

Recommended container size:
40–60 cm across

'Javelin' juncus is ideal for adding a strong sense of architecture because it's the most rigidly straight grass available. It's more like a reed, and like its spiralling cousin is a marginal (water) plant. The Flambe, with its silvery foliage and interspersing growth habit, adds variation in the foliage. The stars of this show, however, are the bright lights of the calibrachoa, lobelia and geraniums.

There's something about the colours here that makes me smile. The two primary and two secondary colours are pure and brash; they know that they're beautiful and that they work well together. Put this container where it can be seen from all around the yard, but don't keep it too close to your sitting area; the colours aren't exactly subtle.

Groupings of containers are the perfect place to use lots of colour.

🅐 Juncus 'Javelin'

Juncus pallidus; common rush

Like its curly cousin 'Spiralis' juncus, 'Javelin' is a water plant that has recently been discovered for its value as a container plant. The only drawback is that juncus needs be kept moist all the time, so when pairing it with drought-resistant plants such as million bells and Flambe, I recommend keeping it in its pot so you can water it daily, whereas you may only water the rest of the container every few days.

🅑 Zonal geranium

see p. 148

🅒 Calibrachoa 'Superbells Dreamsicle'

Calibrachoa hybrid; million bells

Orange is a bit of a rarity in plants, which may explain why we usually can't take our eyes off of it when we see it. 'Dreamsicle' boasts rich, almost creamy orange flowers on robust plants that bloom all summer long. Keep it in full sun and don't be afraid to pinch it back. It prefers to dry slightly between waterings.

🅓 Lobelia 'Laguna Sky Blue'

Lobelia erinus; Indian tobacco

The Laguna Series has the best growth habit of almost any annuals series I've seen. It blooms in round pillows of colour and never seems to stop. Unlike older varieties, 'Laguna Sky Blue' loves the sun.

🅔 Chrysocephalum 'Flambe'

see p. 104

Grouping Containers

If there are several similar things in close proximity to each other, the human eye and brain tends to simplify them and see them as one unit. This tendency can be very helpful in creating a big impact in container design. A grouping of small containers, if they are close together and contain similarly themed ingredients, will appear from a distance as a single unit.

Linda in Vancouver has built a gorgeous grouping into her yard using mostly lobelia, trailing petunias and pansies. By stepping containers

A (above); B (below)

down her stairs toward a larger grouping at the bottom, she creates the illusion of a small river of multi-coloured flowers flowing downward (photo A).

At the Butchart Gardens just outside Victoria, we found a grouping of three containers with identical ingredients (as with planting, I suggest grouping in odd numbers). The effect was impressive, especially because the brocade geraniums in the centres were large enough to overlap each other at points, making it look from above like they were the same plant (photo B).

If you haven't tried grouping your containers before, I strongly suggest playing with the concept. Put some similar containers together, step back and look at them, then try different combinations. A well-done grouping can be a potent weapon in the savvy designer's arsenal.

Lavender Skies

Height: to 1.2 m • **Spread:** to 60 cm

PURPLE IS THE most changeable colour; its mood changes throughout the day as the light changes. This design caught my eye for its innovative use of purples. From the rich, delicious purple of 'Purple Heart' tradescantia to the soft lavender of 'Laguna Heavenly Lilac' lobelia, it's a playful exploration of purples that shows just how well they blend together. I recommend this design or a variation of it for anyone who wants a little more purple in their lives.

Ⓐ Pentas 'Lavender'

Ⓑ Brocade geranium

Ⓒ Tradescantia 'Purple Heart'

Ⓓ Reiger begonia

Ⓔ Lobelia 'Laguna Heavenly Lilac'

Recommended container size:
40–55 cm across

This design uses layers of purples to create a sense of vertical harmony. The central element is a standard 'Lavender' pentas. If you can't find one of these large pentas plants (they can be hard to track down sometimes), the best substitution would be a 'Sun Parasol Pink' mandevilla on a trellis, though that will move the design into more of a pink palette.

What really makes this design work is the harmony of colour and texture in the lower layer. The lobelia and the geraniums blend beautifully together. Both have soft colours and delicate textures, and the lobelia has a sparse enough habit to grow in between the geraniums, which adds to the blending effect. The tradescantia provides the most vibrant colour and adds some excitement to the design; it keeps the elements from becoming too harmonious.

This container would be beautiful as the centrepiece of a grouping of containers. You could pair it with smaller pentas, which are much more readily available. Doing so will provide some difference in shape within the same plant.

Although red is the most popular, pentas come in a variety of colours, with more being introduced all the time.

Ⓐ **Pentas 'Lavender'**

Pentas lanceolata; star flower

Pentas are some of the most stunning annuals to behold when they are in full bloom, but because they don't bloom until late spring or early summer, they are often passed over and left on the benches in May, which is a shame. Put them in the hottest spot possible and fertilize often.

Ⓑ **Brocade geranium**

Pelargonium spp.

Long sidelined at the margins of container gardening, brocade geraniums have burst back onto the scene. They are a softer look than most foliage annuals and are surprisingly versatile and easy to care for. Grow them in full sun or partial shade.

Ⓒ **Tradescantia 'Purple Heart'**

Tradescantia pallida;
inch plant, wandering Jew

This old-fashioned houseplant is stunning in containers. Its thick leaves have gorgeous long lines and a sublime purple colour. Keep them in at least morning sun or the colour will fade. They will need to be acclimatized to afternoon sun in drier regions.

Ⓓ **Reiger begonia**

Begonia x *hiemalis;* Elatior begonia

Reiger begonias are classic houseplants, and this is the first time I've seen one in an outdoor container garden. They produce richly coloured flowers on and off all year as long as you protect them from full sun.

Ⓔ **Lobelia 'Laguna Heavenly Lilac'**
see p. 284

Tree Form Centrepieces

Using a standard plant (i.e., one that has been trained to grow like a tree) as a centrepiece adds a lot of impact to a container. The tree form, with a canopy at the top and a lower layer of filler plants, is an effective recreation of nature. Standard form plants can, however, be difficult to track down. Call your favourite large garden centre if you're interested and ask if they will be

A (above left); B (above right)

carrying any standard annuals in the spring. I advise against trying to form them yourself; it takes a lot of time and will probably only lead to frustration.

One of my favourite things about this design style is that the centrepiece takes up almost no space at soil level, so you can pile the fillers in around it and make the composition look much larger than the container would suggest.

Butchart Gardens outside Victoria had several tree form designs. A monochromatic white container with a gorgeous sweet potato vine centrepiece and trailing petunias spilling out the sides of it caught my eye (photo A).

If you can find it, heliotrope is an ideal candidate for the centrepiece of a tree form design. Elevating the flowers closer to nose level makes their irresistible scent that much stronger to the passer-by (photo B).

Calypso

Height: to 50 cm · **Spread:** to 70 cm

WHEN IT COMES to colour combinations, yellow on black is the most eye-catching contrast around. This contemporary design is meant to excite the eyes and stir the senses. Warm, sunshine yellows in traditional cottage shapes clash vividly, almost violently, against stark, glossy, black lines. This recipe will make a great conversation piece in a garden with a modern theme, but its colours are so stimulating that I suggest using it sparingly.

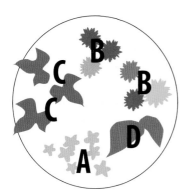

Ⓐ Bidens 'Solaire Yellow'

Ⓑ Bracteantha 'Sundaze Flame'

Ⓒ Sweet potato vine 'Sweet
Caroline Purple'

Ⓓ Coleus

Recommended container size:
30–45 cm across

While the contrasting colours provide the bulk of the impact, the shapes play a part, as well. Bidens are one of the most vivid yellows available, and their old-fashioned, daisy-like shape adds even more contrast against the dark, jagged and serrated foliage of sweet potato vine. You can play with these shapes and colours at will, muting or amplifying the amount of contrast like dials on a stereo.

You'll want to put this design in the full sun so its colours stay as vibrant as possible. It's up to you how compact you want to keep it; you could keep trimming back the bidens and sweet potato vine or just let them grow. If you want to add even more visual impact, try a 'Jurassic Dark' alocasia or even some dwarf sunflowers. Note that the pot is yellow; with a design this devoted to the impact of colour, it's natural to use a brightly coloured pot.

This design is an example of how too much contrast can cause overstimulation and a sense of chaos. I suggest grouping this potent container with other, simpler containers, perhaps either all black or all yellow using some of the same ingredients, to give the eye a place to relax.

Sunflowers are one of my favourite flowers for their pure, honest joy that will never go out of style.

🅐 **Bidens 'Solaire Yellow'**

Bidens ferulifolia; beggartick

I recommend 'Solaire' for this design because it stays much more compact than many other varieties and is really more of a filler plant than a trailer. Fertilize it liberally and don't be shy about trimming it back after a bout of cool, cloudy weather. It will grow back even fuller when the sun comes out.

🅑 **Bracteantha 'Sundaze Flame'**

Helichrysum bracteatum;
golden everlasting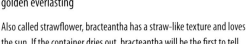

Also called strawflower, bracteantha has a straw-like texture and loves the sun. If the container dries out, bracteantha will be the first to tell you. Its leaves droop as if dying at the first hint of drought, but ironically it's remarkably drought tolerant and bounces back nicely.

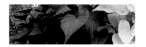

🅒 **Sweet potato vine 'Sweet Caroline Purple'**
see p. 92

🅓 **Coleus**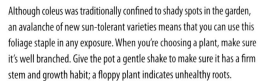

Solenostemon hybrida; flame nettle

Although coleus was traditionally confined to shady spots in the garden, an avalanche of new sun-tolerant varieties means that you can use this foliage staple in any exposure. When you're choosing a plant, make sure it's well branched. Give the pot a gentle shake to make sure it has a firm stem and growth habit; a floppy plant indicates unhealthy roots.

Designing with Yellow

Yellow is the colour of a field of ripe canola, of sunflowers towering out of the garden and of bright pansies grinning back at you. It's the happiest colour, and when you have a lot of yellow in the garden it's impossible not to smile a little when you're strolling through. It's so warm that it can often seem out of place in very contemporary designs. I usually recommend using it in more traditional designs or, even better, on its own.

Vera Popnik uses yellow around her front door to great effect. The yellow flowers are the unifying force amongst all the containers, especially the bright bidens sprinkled down the front steps and under the window

A (above); B (below)

like a host of fireflies on a summer's night. The yellow is also the first thing on which the eye focuses (photo A).

Yellow pansies are perhaps the most cheerful flowers in the world. We found a unique container that blended their bright faces with the broad, cream stripes of a variegated hosta in a cozy whisky barrel (photo B).

Summer Cocktail

Height: to 1 m • **Spread:** to 70 cm

I'M AMAZED AT how differently people act when shopping for annuals as opposed to shrubs. In the annuals area, they are usually curious and eager to try new things, always asking, "How about this one?" Once in the shrubs, it's down to business. Shrubs are serious stuff, and the question becomes, "How big will this be in 10 years?" Annuals evoke a sense of fun and creativity; shrubs evoke commitment and careful planning, and that's a shame because shrubs are as striking in containers as annuals are.

A Weigela 'Wine & Roses'

B Gaura 'Karalee Petite Pink'

C Phlox 'Intensia White'

D Petunia 'Supertunia Vista Bubblegum'

Recommended container size:
45–60 cm across

Shrubs are ideal for containers because they are not very expensive when compared to very large annuals (often only a little bit more), and they bring an instant sense of bulk to your container, making them impressive in May when everything else is just waking up. Choose a shrub for its foliage because shrub flowering is usually short lived and will be drowned out by the braggart annuals.

This container will thrive in full sun all summer as the annuals grow into the shrub. The delicate, lacy gaura blooms will weave in and out of the broad, purple weigela leaves for a wonderful effect while the larger-flowered petunias and phlox will provide the bulk of the pizzazz.

Even though it usually won't survive the winter in a pot, a container shrub doesn't need to be disposable. If you fall in love with one over summer and want to keep it, simply remove it from the container (carefully, and with as large a root mass as possible so as not to hurt its root system) and plant it in the ground. This way you get a grand show in a container while slowly filling your yard year after year. Make sure you give it some time to establish itself when transplanting; mid-fall will be fine as long as you water it in well. If you leave the shrub in the container, it probably won't survive winter unless the container is very large or you submerge the pot in effective winter mulch.

'My Monet' weigela would be a unique twist to a container with a shrub.

A Weigela 'Wine & Roses'
Weigela florida

This full, richly coloured shrub loves to soak up the sun. Regular fertilizing will keep the foliage a rich, dark backdrop to frame and highlight the lighter colours of the annuals. The broad leaves also provide textural contrast with the gaura, making the container a delight to look it.

B Gaura 'Karalee Petite Pink'
Gaura lindheimeri; butterfly flower

It's gorgeous wherever it goes, but with the weigela accenting it, the soft pink flowers almost seem like they're in flight.

C Phlox 'Intensia White'
Phlox drummondii; Drummond phlox

The white phlox brings a stark colour contrast with the weigela that adds a sense of modernity to the design. If you want a container with harmonious colours while keeping the dynamic textures, then take out the phlox or replace it with pink verbena.

D Petunia 'Supertunia Vista Bubblegum'
see p. 172

Using Shrubs in Containers

Using shrubs as centrepieces gives containers an instant "wow" factor that no annual can match, especially in spring and early summer when the annuals haven't fully matured. Savvy gardeners who have garden parties or events before mid-July often use shrubs to give a sense of maturity to their container designs. Shrubs will also make a simple recipe look daring because people aren't used to seeing them in containers. A sprinkling of pansies and sweet potato vine isn't much on its own,

A (bottom left); B (above); C (below)

but add a crisp evergreen and people do a double-take (photo A).

My stepmother paired a wire vine *(Muehlenbeckia)* with a tea-rose for a simple yet dramatic combination. Tea-roses make lovely container plants (especially in colder regions where they often die over winter), and the vine adds a complementing texture while covering the unsightly soil (photo B).

Another great shrub for containers is butterfly bush *(Buddleia)*. Its purple spires add a dramatic sense of architecture that provides visual appeal as

well as attracting butterflies, bees and even hummingbirds if you have them in your area (photo C).

The Licorice Tower

Height: to 1.5 m • **Spread:** to 60 cm

THIS CONTAINER HAPPENED via a very happy accident. One day in the back greenhouses I found some cilantro that had been planted in a herb pot and forgotten. It had grown to be over 1 metre tall with dozens of white flower clusters exploding into a canopy. I was smitten and just had to see what it looked like in a recipe, so I ran about the greenhouse collecting ingredients. The result was a true statement maker, a white recipe with both harmonious and contrasting textures within it.

- Ⓐ Cilantro
- Ⓑ Hosta 'Patriot'
- Ⓒ Papyrus 'King Tut'
- Ⓓ Gaura 'Stratosphere White'
- Ⓔ Lobelia 'Laguna White'
- Ⓕ Asparagus fern

Recommended container size:
  40–50 cm wide

There is a lot to see here. I used the 'King Tut' papyrus and the gaura to provide a bridge for the eye between the cilantro canopy and the explosion of texture below. 'King Tut's' straight stalks also bring a sense of rigidity and architecture to the otherwise flowing vertical lines.

The cilantro rises like a cloud while the lobelia and asparagus fern unite the canopy with the bottom of the container. The hosta acts as a secondary focal point, with its broad, bold leaves rising out of the lacy texture.

I love the subtle blend of greens, from the rich green hosta and lobelia to the lime green asparagus fern. The use of white, however, is my favourite thing about the design. Often white is all big, broad flowers that lack a sense of movement. This design brings out the fresh, playful side of white.

This container is easy to care for in partial sun (the lobelia and hosta appreciate afternoon shade). The cilantro is the wild card. It grows too tall for its own good, prompting me to use the curly willow on either side of it. More than just a vertical accent to add an intriguing form, the willow is woven into the unstable cilantro as a support stake. You may occasionally have to clean the brown leaves from the lower half of the cilantro.

This container uses a large willow as the centrepiece. Flanked by fuchsia and sweet potato vine, it creates a monstrous, contrasting creation.

Ⓐ Cilantro

Coriandrum sativum

Nothing special here—it's the plain-jane, potted herb cilantro that is easily available. It grows quickly, and once it blooms, if you squeeze the flowers between your fingers the smell is unmistakably licorice. It will need some subtle support; I find curly willow works best because it's much more ornamental than a trellis and enhances the sense of wild texture.

Ⓑ Hosta 'Patriot'

Hosta spp.

Its broad leaves create a striking harmony with the delicate plants around it. Although you may eventually have to protect it from the faster growing lobelia, its effect of reaching over the other plants like protective hands and holding them down will intrigue the eye.

Ⓒ Papyrus 'King Tut'
see p. 284

Gaura 'Stratosphere White'
see p. 184

Ⓔ Lobelia 'Laguna White'
see p. 112

Ⓕ Asparagus fern
see p. 100

Designs for Narrow Spaces

You can make a high-impact container even if your space is very limited. "The Licorice Tower" featured here packs a lot of visual appeal, but from a square space perspective it's remarkably compact. If you're dealing with a small space, it's important that you find the right ingredients.

Look for a tall, narrow pot. A short and narrow pot will look small, but tall pots often have a modern flair.

Choose ingredients that are tall with a width that's disproportionate to their height; tall, narrow plants will make the width of the space look larger,

A (above); B (below)

compared to wide, short plants that will do the opposite. Carrie Hamilton used 'Purple Majesty' millet in an ornate urn to achieve a sense of height. To add to the effect she added 'Wojo's Gem' vinca, which hangs straight down with almost no width. This combination encourages the eye to travel in an unbroken vertical line up the elements (photo A).

Urns are ideal for narrow-space designing. Their tapering forms and narrow necks encourage tall, thin ingredients (photo B).

Poker Face

Height: to 1 m • **Spread:** to 50 cm

IF YOU HAVE A TASTE for the macabre, this shadowy composition might be just the thing to put a little midnight in your garden. The mass of black leaves pulls the eye through layers of darkness while the wicked orange mouths of the thunbergia cackle at you. The harmonious darkness is intoxicating, and the contrasting textures of the leaves enhance the effect. It's an eye-catcher to be sure.

A Millet 'Purple Baron'

B Alternanthera 'Purple Knight'

C Sweet potato vine 'Sweet Caroline Purple'

D Thunbergia 'Sunny'

Recommended container size:
35–45 cm across

This recipe breaks several unwritten rules of container gardening. The only flowering colour is in the trailing vine, necessitating a tall, preferably narrow container. The thunbergia is a climbing vine that usually has a trellis attached to it, but like many vines, if you don't give it anything to climb, it will trail down in long strands and is probably the best orange trailer around.

As the summer scorches on, the sweet potato vine and the alternanthera will add substantial bulk to the mix and make the design seem wild and maybe a little out of control. Use a large container because all the ingredients will grow quickly.

A sunny spot is best for this recipe, especially one where it can gather shadows as twilight falls. The only thing that might need rescuing is the alternanthera from the thunbergia. The latter may grab the former and try to use it for leverage to climb upward.

Ample fertilizer will ensure that the container keeps performing for you.

'Sunny' thunbergia makes such striking contrast with black sweet potato vine that it's almost jarring to look at.

A Millet 'Purple Baron'

Pennisetum glaucum; ornamental millet

'Purple Baron' is a more compact version of the original 'Purple Majesty.' The blades are broader and turn a rich purple the more sun and heat you give them. It will send up tightly bound plumes that turn to seed and attract birds from late summer through fall.

B Alternanthera 'Purple Knight'

Alternanthera dentata; blood leaf

An under-appreciated foliage vine, alternanthera will really impress in full sun. If you want to take advantage of the subtle red tones in the leaves, as well as add more colour to the body of the recipe, try adding some red trailing verbena to the mix (for instance, 'Tukana Scarlet').

C Sweet potato vine 'Sweet Caroline Purple'
see p. 92

D Thunbergia 'Sunny'

Thunbergia alata; black-eyed Susan vine

Blooming like crazy in the summer heat, 'Sunny' is a terrific improvement on the original black-eyed Susan vine. It's exciting to see it used as a trailing plant. If you want to jazz up the recipe with more contrast (and make it a little less dark in tone), try using orange and yellow varieties together instead of just orange.

Using Climbing Vines as Trailers

Gardening is about creativity, and nothing is written in stone. We think that we need to put a climbing vine on a trellis because it's always been done like that, but when we think outside the box we see that climbing vines can look just as good (or even better) when they're made to trail. You're designing living, breathing compositions; consider every plant a possible ingredient and try to imagine the role it can play with fresh eyes and regardless of the role it normally plays.

You can often discover the hidden habits of plants when you train them to grow in different ways. Scarlet runner bean is one of my favourite vines, but I didn't appreciate how eye-catching the individual vines were (I had only ever seen them en masse) until I saw

A (above); B (below)

it being used as a trailing vine (photo A).

Sweet pea is another vine that makes a beautiful trailer. When allowed to cascade, its messy habit and upward-arcing flowers make it look like a wave striking the ground and splashing upward (photo B). Its greedy tendrils will create tension in the container as they grab their neighbours and attempt to pull themselves up in an effort to climb.

Parasol

Height: to 1 m • **Spread:** to 1 m

WITH SO MANY high-performance annuals available today, it's easy to get addicted to using masses of colour at the cost of more elegant compositions. This recipe uses cool colour harmonies and intriguing textural twists to fashion a classical, almost Victorian focal point. Although it would be striking anywhere, it would look especially good in the centre of a patio with other elegant, cool containers. This is a container to build your yard around.

A Juniper 'Blue Prince'

B Fescue 'Elijah Blue'

C Cobbity daisy

D Artemisia

E Lamb's ear

Recommended container size:
60–90 cm across

The elegance of this design comes from a mix of classical looking ingredients and a harmonic, cool colour scheme to relax the eye. It's a sophisticated palette of blues, whites and silvers. Silver tones are excellent daylight extenders, catching the sun and throwing it back after sunset like solar lights.

The bust finishes it off nicely. Don't be shy about using a favourite heirloom (or a new favourite) in a container to help better articulate the story you want to tell. Just make sure that it can handle some sunlight and the occasional watering.

This container will tolerate anything from morning to full sun. Since most of the ingredients are slow-growing, it's almost maintenance free. If you do have only morning sun, try substituting white double impatiens for the cobbities. If you can't get one or two of the ingredients, don't be afraid to add harmonic stuffers such as lotus vine, sage, blue echeveria or bacopa.

A tree-form centrepiece creates an alluring canopy above the lower sections of the container.

Ⓐ Juniper 'Blue Prince' (grafted)
Juniperus horizontalis

Rarely found in containers, this juniper plays the role of an umbrella shading a proper Victorian lady from the garish sun. Standards are usually expensive, so try to find a home for it in your garden in fall.

Ⓑ Fescue 'Elijah Blue'
see p. 156

Ⓒ Cobbity daisy
Argyranthemum frutescens; Marguerite daisy

Double white cobbities are a delight in containers and don't tend to get as weedy looking as their single white cousins (although they don't bloom as much, either). If they do get leggy (the only thing in this recipe that would), don't be afraid to give them a haircut and some fertilizer; there's plenty more here to entertain the eye.

Ⓓ Artemisia
Artemisia spp.; wormwood

Long known for its medicinal properties, artemisia is also an ornamental perennial with finely textured, silvery foliage and a habit that resembles a messy haircut. It doesn't need much fertilizer, is drought tolerant, and is almost completely maintenance free.

Ⓔ Lamb's ear
see p. 104

Using Fountains as Planters

The feature ("Parasol") uses several elements to give it an elegantly Victorian look. The umbrella-like juniper, combined with the classic bust, makes the viewer think of taking a young lady for a turn around the estate's garden (with a chaperone, of course). The cool palette of the plants adds to the sense of decorum.

A (left)

B (above left); C (above right)

I love the use of the old concrete water fountain as a planter. If you have an old water fountain or bird bath that you want to revitalize, or if it's cracked and leaks water, then try turning it into a conversation-starting container garden. The only thing to remember with using an old fountain or birdbath is, that unless the bowl is cracked or you can find drainage (many fountains will drain from the centre where the pump went once you peel off the sealant), you will need to be careful not to drown your poor plants. A thick layer of stones underneath the soil will help with drainage.

A fountain design can be anything you want it to be. At Wellington Garden Centre in Edmonton we found some striking examples, including a lovely annuals garden with a soft citrus palette (photo A).

A bed of succulents, if done right, gives the illusion of a forest floor teeming with strange plant life bursting out everywhere (photos B and C).

Forest Fire

Height: to 1 m · **Spread:** to 1.2 m

TURN ON THE SUMMER heat for this one! Filled with vibrant sun lovers, this recipe will explode in the blazing July and August heat. Everything here is as warm and exciting as a forest fire. While the black elder contrasts vividly in colour and texture with the million bells, the fiery colours of the lantana add a splash Mediterranean heat. As the elder grows larger and the reds and yellows of the flowers billow like plumes of flame, it will be sensational when everything else is panting in the heat.

Ⓐ Black elder

Ⓑ Lantana 'Lucky Red Flame'

Ⓒ Calibrachoa 'Superbells Apricot Punch'

Recommended container size:
60–75 cm across

Perfect for a scorching south- or west-facing deck or a fully exposed patio, the plants in this recipe need to stay hot but aren't overly drought tolerant, so keep the hose handy. The elder is a shrub that will fill out nicely over the season and, assuming it's hot enough, the lantana will fill the spaces between the elder's spare branches.

If you want more trailing appeal than the calibrachoa hanging over the side, try adding a dark vine, such as an 'Illusion' sweet potato vine, that has shapes that will harmonize with the elder and will draw the container together vertically.

Although it will light up the yard in August, I would keep some cooler season containers handy nearby that will wow until then. If you want to make a grouping with a couple of other heat lovers, try some smaller pots of lantana or calibrachoa around it. Fertilize it liberally so it can be at its best when the heat arrives.

'Black Lace' sambucus has heavily serrated leaves and boasts playful light purple flower clusters in mid-summer.

Ⓐ Black elder
Sambucus nigra

A lot of people think of shrubs as boring and green, but in the past decade, varieties have been introduced with as much colour and flair for design as any exotic annual. Black elder, with its highly serrated leaves and black foliage, is a perfect example. It's hardy in many regions, so plant it out in early fall if you want to keep it.

Ⓑ Lantana 'Lucky Red Flame'
Lantana camara; shrub verbena

With some of the most vivid colour in the garden, the only thing stopping lantana from becoming one of the most popular annuals in Canada is its addiction to heat, of which we receive precious little. It also loves humidity and tends to perform best in hot, humid regions. It has a pungent aroma, so I don't recommend putting it too close to your sitting area.

Ⓒ Calibrachoa 'Superbells Apricot Punch'
Calibrachoa hybrid; million bells

Planting million bells is one of the best ways there is to look like a gardening genius. They grow like crazy in full sun and are at their best in containers that throw subtlety out the window and are all about big colour. If the summer is cool and wet, they will start to get leggy. Trim them back and hope for warmer, drier days in September.

The Best Shrubs for your Designs

Hardy shrubs typically bloom only once a year, so if you're thinking of using one for a container design, I suggest choosing one whose best feature is its foliage. Richly coloured or exquisitely shaped leaves will look great all season, while a bloom may be remarkable for a few weeks but then fade, leaving you with plain green leaves.

The elder in the featured design is an excellent choice and comes in several varieties. It's also winter hardy (though a bit tender) on the Prairies. If you live in a warmer region, your options for container shrubs broaden dramatically. Japanese maples, a lower Ontario favourite, often come in a deliciously rich red and boast delicate, strikingly serrated leaves. Combine one with a canna lily and purple fountain grass, and the result is a design that bombards the eye with intense textural contrast (photo A).

A (above); B (below)

Japanese maples bring a vividly delicate, Oriental feel to containers. If
you are in a colder climate and your
thumb is well and truly green, you
can overwinter one in a cold space
with a lot of light (photo B).

Night at the Opera

Height: to 70 cm · **Spread:** to 50 cm

I STUDIED THE ROMANTICS as an undergrad and was fascinated with the brilliant angst of poets such as Blake and Goethe and how their poems, though often dark and brooding, could also be triumphant and bold. This container reminded me of them. To me it feels both intimate and epic, nightmarish and unabashedly heroic. The container and the textures of the unorthodox ingredients work together to make you realize that looking at a stunning container and reading a brilliant poem aren't that different after all.

A Phormium 'Amazing Red'

B Sempervivum

C String of pearls

Recommended container size:
30–45 cm across

This recipe is about bold, crisp lines and radically contrasting textures. While the shining, lance-like blades of the phormium soar overhead, the sempervivums huddle below, like medieval pilgrims in awe of supernatural forces.

Much of this composition's appeal is in the container. I suggest looking for an impressive container when you plant this recipe because its minimalist design and lack of significant trailers very much makes the container a part of the recipe.

Best as a sunny focal point, possibly in the middle of a large table or platform, this container is almost completely maintenance free and likes to dry out significantly between waterings. You don't have to cram the sempervivum in too tightly; its pups will spread quickly to fill every open spot. Before long they will be jostling for more space while the phormium stretches into the sky.

Cryptanthus (earth stars) is a strange and unique ingredient for small containers.

Ⓐ Phormium 'Amazing Red'

Phormium tenax; New Zealand flax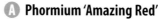

Phormium has a unique relationship with light. At night, the blades will turn melancholy and black, as if the sempervivums below have angered them. When the sun catches them in the day, however, they shimmer with light. It is a great plant to bring indoors in fall because it grows thicker and larger with each year and is fairly expensive. Make sure to submerge the pot instead of transplanting and to wipe the blades down with insecticidal soap before bringing it indoors.

Ⓑ Sempervivum

Sempervivum tectorum; hens and chicks

These are common hens and chicks (a darker variety), but there are any number of sempervivums, with a variety of colours and textures, that you can use. If you make the effort to transplant the pups, they also make low-maintenance houseplants or perennials that can be used in containers year after year.

Ⓒ String of pearls

Senecio herreianus

This very old-fashioned houseplant is beginning to be rediscovered for the design potential of its spherical bulbs. Although you may have to shop around, it's worth the effort. It's a slow-growing succulent that doesn't like much water.

Designing for Drama

It can be intimidating sometimes to plant such a bold design, but the rewards are well worth it. Despite its unique appearance, this grasses-and-succulents style is surprisingly easy to care for. The ingredients don't need to be cut back and are drought tolerant.

If you want a similar look but in a smaller space, perhaps as a centrepiece, replacing the phormium with dwarf fountain grass (*Pennisetum setaceum* 'Red Riding Hood') is an easy variation (photo A). There are so many different sempervivums that you can choose your colour and texture.

You can add more colour to the mix by using red cobbity daisies and white euphorbia around the phormium (photo B). Although this mix isn't as brooding, the filler plants are still dramatic enough to make an

A (above); B (below)

impression, and it will fit easier into a less contemporary garden.

With no fillers in this recipe, much of the appeal will depend on your choice of container. Don't be afraid to try a dramatic container. It's your garden, after all, and your designs should be an expression of your personality, no matter how bold that makes them.

French Countryside

Height: to 40 cm • **Spread:** to 1.5 m

THIS CONTAINER USES some high-performance ingredients to capture an old-world, European charm. It's one of the few recipes that can grow to an eye-catching, impressive size while still maintaining an intimate, cozy feel. When I saw it, I thought of Quebec and many of the window boxes that I've seen throughout that beautiful province. It would look brilliant in a yard with classic themes and colours.

A Boxwood

B Begonia 'Illumination Salmon Pink'

C Lamium 'Pink Chablis'

Recommended container size:
30 cm by 90 cm

Like many great designs, the recipe isn't as simple as it seems. The charm comes from the understated harmonies of the subtle pink lamium flowers blending with the pink begonias and the arrowhead shapes of the leaves on both plants.

The boxwood in the back, though it doesn't brag, adds greatly to the European charm. In warmer regions you can plant the boxwood as a shrub in fall. In colder regions you may have to hunt around to find it.

If you have a wooden window box with a lot of character to it, this recipe will fit in nicely. You'll need to protect it from the afternoon sun, especially in drier regions, and fertilize regularly to keep the begonia leaves a rich green.

This recipe would also group nicely with a patio pot or two that use almost the same ingredients, possibly substituting a flowering annual like double impatiens or upright fuchsia for the lamium to give it more of a presence.

Lavender is a classic beauty that brings to mind images of the French countryside.

A Boxwood
Buxus sempervirens; European boxwood

Arguably the most well-known hedge shrub in the world, its tight habit and glossy leaves make it a fitting (though possibly expensive) addition to a window box celebrating classic themes in gardening. Protect it from the afternoon sun.

B Begonia 'Illumination Salmon Pink'
Begonia x *hybrida;* trailing begonia

Some of the most exciting introductions in the past few years have been trailing begonias. In sheltered heat these tropical beauties will bloom all summer, the pendulums dancing in every strong breeze. As with upright begonias, pinch the single flowers (the male flowers) so there's no hanky-panky, which leads to the plant going to seed.

C Lamium 'Pink Chablis'
Lamium maculatum; dead nettle

Lamium is an old favourite that has been recently reintroduced as a more compact, vigorous container stuffer. The multiple colours on each leaf add interest while subtle, soft pink flower clusters harmonize with the begonias.

Creating Themed Groupings

The most amazing gardens usually start with a theme around which the gardener builds the designs. The feature window box was only one element of a themed area that we discovered at Wellington Garden Centre in Edmonton. They had designed a series of containers of various sizes to create a scene that could have been taken right out of rural Provence (photo B).

In any themed grouping, not every design needs to be complicated. In this book I've typically highlighted what would be the most complicated

A (bottom left); B (above)

container in a theme. To finish the theme, build simpler containers around it. In the French area at Wellington, one container was a simple, small boxwood wreathed in sphagnum moss.

If you want a little less quaint and a little more flair for your window box, consider adding some foliage plants with more flash than lamium and

boxwood. A good variation is 'Kong' coleus and heuchera (photo A).

One themed container surrounded by completely different designs may seem out of place. Surround it with designs in the same theme; even if it's a container with just one ingredient for accent, suddenly you've created a tiny other world in your garden.

Begonia Surprise

Height: to 1 m • **Spread:** to 1.5 m

THERE HAVE BEEN a lot of exciting introductions in trailing tuberous begonias over the last few years, giving gardeners who love these big tropic beauties more options for hot, sunny spots. This container was designed to harmonize the textures of the begonias with the phormium and the colours of the begonias with the iresine. What it became, however, was the perfect opportunity for the voracious begonia to stretch its dense flower clusters into the sun and claim the container for itself.

Ⓐ Phormium

Ⓑ Begonia 'Million Kisses'

Ⓒ Iresine 'Blazin Rose'

Ⓓ Purple fountain grass 'Fireworks'

Ⓔ English ivy

Recommended container size:
   60–75 cm across

The begonia's favourite hobby is devouring every other plant around it. Its ravenous growth habit makes it a victim of its own success because it limits its versatility in mixed containers. The fountain grass, iresine and English ivy were almost the same size as the begonias when this container was planted. In this picture, taken only mid-way through a hot July, you can almost hear them begging for mercy. But the phormium, escaping the chaos, thrives.

This beefy container showcases the 'Million Kisses' variety at its very best. 'Million Kisses,' along with many of the new trailing begonias, can handle full sun, though you should watch for burning of the leaves in drier regions. Watering begonias can be tricky; they aren't drought tolerant, but leaving the soil surface wet may bring on powdery mildew. If they're in a warm, breezy spot, mildew shouldn't be a problem.

If you can't find 'Million Kisses,' 'Bonfire' begonias are an excellent substitute.

Here, begonias blend with heuchera and phormium to create a container that's charming in its messiness.

Ⓐ Phormium

Phormium tenax; New Zealand flax

The messy verticality and sleek colours of a phormium seem to fit in anywhere! If you plan to keep yours year after year, make sure to submerge the pot in the soil to protect its roots from the begonia.

Ⓑ Begonia 'Million Kisses'

Begonia x *hybrida;* trailing begonia

Fairly new to the market but very impressive, sun-loving, trailing begonias can take full sun (if tempered with a little humidity, either from the air or from the hose) and grow quickly to fill out a basket. This single-flowering, semi-trailing variety is low maintenance and doesn't require deadheading. As long as you fertilize it generously and give it ample sunlight, it never seems to stop blooming!

Ⓒ Iresine 'Blazin Rose'
see p. 80

Ⓓ Purple fountain grass 'Fireworks'

Pennisetum setaceum; red fountain grass

This remarkably coloured fountain grass is fairly new but is already very popular with savvy gardeners looking for more vibrant grasses. Although it will not grow as tall as its purple cousins, its rich red blades and less aggressive growth habit make it an ideal eye-catcher in many kinds of recipes.

Ⓔ English ivy
see p. 312

Heat-loving Foliage

There's a lot more out there for foliage fillers than coleus, especially if you live in a warmer region of Canada. As soon as the spring nights stay above 8° Celsius, the heat-loving foliage plants will start to branch out and will become very aggressive in the summer heat.

If you're in a cooler climate, like the Prairies or the North, and are shopping for foliage plants, check the back of the tag to see what zone it's from; if it's zone 11 or 12, it won't perform well in the chilly May nights.

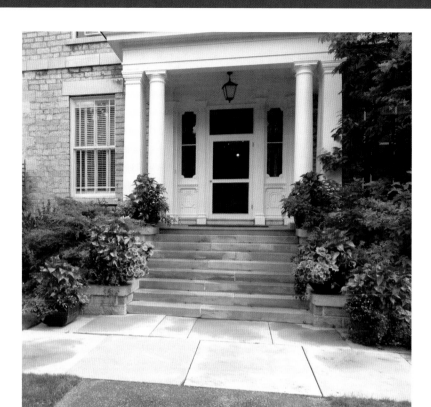

A (above); B (below)

At Rideau Hall, the groundskeeper uses copperleaf (*Acalypha* spp.) in containers lining the steps up to the guest residence (photo A). It's a stunner in Ottawa, but I would think twice about using it in Calgary or Regina, where it won't really start to perform until into June.

Iresine (also called beefsteak plant) is another tropical stunner that loves the heat (photo B). Its distinct, crisply variegated leaves make it a show-stopper, and it grows very large when the summer sun gets intense. When shopping for iresine, look for plants that are well branched.

Taking Flight

Height: to 80 cm · **Spread:** to 80 cm

SOME OF THE BEST designs are those that pulse with a sense of movement, as if at any moment they could leap from their root anchors and escape into the garden. Here, in the airy spires of the gaura and the fluttering sweet potato vine, I can almost see a flock of pink birds disturbed and leaping into the air, filling the sky with the organized chaos of flapping wings. Designs can be more than just beautiful; they can also express a vivid sense of kinetic engergy.

A Gaura 'Karalee Petite Pink'

B Heuchera 'Dolce Creme Brulee'

C Sweet potato vine 'Tricolor'

Recommended container size:
35–45 cm across

The sense of movement I see here comes from a combination of the gaura vaulting and weaving upward and the loose, fluttering habit of the sweet potato vine leaves. The heuchera stabilizes the scene while a host of winged leaves and flowers fly from its branches.

If you want to add even more movement to this container, try adding trailing pink nemesia or a soft pink verbena to the mix. Both will cascade over the sides, and their body and slightly upward–arching stems will add nicely to the kinetic energy already built in.

Don't be afraid to experiment with creating movement in your original designs. Look for plants that pulse with a sense of energy on the garden centre bench, and go from there.

I recommend putting this container in the middle of the yard in an exposed spot where every gust of wind will flutter its leaves and flowers. Although it doesn't boast vibrant contrasting colours or pillows of flowers falling over the edge, the quiet sense of joy that you will feel when you look at it makes it a stirring focal point.

Digitalis (foxglove) will bring a sense of movement to a design.

Ⓐ Gaura 'Karalee Petite Pink'

Gaura lindheimeri; butterfly flower

One of my favourite newer annuals, gaura brings a sense of energy and movement. 'Karalee Petite Pink' is the shorter variety. If you want to add even more wings to the flock, try adding the taller and lighter pink 'Stratosphere Pink Picotee' to the mix. Keep gaura in full sun.

Ⓑ Heuchera 'Dolce Creme Brulee'

Heuchera spp.; coral bells

Heuchera is an old-fashioned favourite that has found its niche in 21st-century gardening. Newer varieties with glossy black or warm orange leaves are transforming how we think about this once passive perennial—from quiet flower bed stuffer to trendy design ingredient.

Ⓒ Sweet potato vine 'Tricolor'

Ipomoea batatas

Although not nearly as famous or as fast growing as its lime cousin, 'Tricolor' still comes in handy in designs thanks to its unique, soft pink variegation. Like all sweet potato vines, try to keep the soil slightly moist, and fertilize generously.

Designing for Movement

Achieving a sense of movement in container design can be elusive, but once you do it, the rewards are breathtaking! A design that flutters with life in the breeze will lift your mood whenever you look at it. The negative things we feel at the end of a hard day, like stress and frustration, are all downward-spiralling emotions. To come home at the end of that day and see designs that vault upward into the sky can be a wonderful way to lift your spirits.

A (bottom left); B (above)

Most plants that inspire a sense of movement have a sparse growth habit so that they can grow upward in between other stuffers with a relaxed, gentle habit.

Flambe is a great ingredient for providing a sense of movement. Its powdered silver branches are always arcing upward out of the container as if reaching for the sky. Each branch is topped with a densely bundled, bright yellow flower that catches the sun just right on a bright day (photo A).

Along the Victoria harbour, Meg and I saw some incredible moss baskets with dainty pink flowers exploding out from all around them (photo B). The magical ingredient was an old-fashioned annual called viscaria. On its own, viscaria is often too stringy and large to be very attractive. Cleverly planted in these baskets, however, where it could grow between the other plants and burst out in every direction, it provided a stunning sense of movement that I couldn't take my eyes off of.

Jester

Height: to 40 cm · **Spread:** to 50 cm

IT'S USUALLY EASIER than you think to give traditional flowers a modern twist. New Guinea impatiens are an established standby, especially in humid regions, but juncus has only recently begun to be widely used in container design. As you can see, juncus gives this simple recipe a stirring and invigorating sense of architectural movement. With the sparse juncus growing between the New Guinea stems, it will seem as if a single strange new plant has been born in your yard!

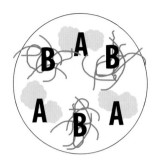

New Guinea impatiens
'Infinity Pink Frost'

Juncus 'Spiralis'

Recommended container size:
25–40 cm across

My first reaction when I saw this container was, "Why didn't I think of that?" The juncus beautifully emphasizes and amplifies the roundness of the flowers and the contrasting dark leaves of the impatiens. In designing with plants, the simpler options often produce the best results. Two dance partners with great chemistry will always look better on stage than an exhaustingly choreographed routine with dancers who don't have good chemistry with each other.

Juncus is not a big plant, and the subtle shapes and delicate corkscrews will be best enjoyed near your favourite sitting area. The beauty is that the composition is so simple that you can make as small (one plant of each) or as large a container as you like.

I recommend trying a grouping of this design, perhaps in a variety of New Guinea colours. If you want to experiment within this easy model, try substituting double impatiens for New Guineas, or try adding some torenia or scaevola to the mix.

New Guinea impatiens aren't sun intolerant as much as they are dry air intolerant. In Miami they are a favourite boulevard plant, growing in full sun in the middle of searing hot tarmac. In dry regions of Canada, however, the afternoon scorch will burn holes through their tropical leaves. If you live in a humid region, try exposing New Guineas to some afternoon sun, but watch for tell-tale brown burn marks.

Pink diascia has a playful innocence that would make for an intriguing textural blend with juncus.

A **New Guinea impatiens 'Infinity Pink Frost'**

Impatiens x hawkeri; busy Lizzie

Recent varieties of New Guineas bloom so relentlessly and stay so compact that their "wow" factor now competes with the very showiest of annuals. Their passionate colours and glossy leaves cry out tropical. Make sure the soil is always slightly moist; they will pout if you make them wilt. Don't worry about getting a particular variety; just look for healthy, well-branched plants.

B **Juncus 'Spiralis'**

Juncus effusus; corkscrew rush

Although juncus was once considered only a water garden plant, keen gardeners with an eye for contemporary designs have snapped up this sassy little plant to act as architectural jester in their containers. It grows slowly, so you may want to keep it in its pot and bring it indoors in fall. Make sure it's always kept moist.

Juncus the Jester

The feature container ("Jester") works because it adds a literal twist to an established favourite. This is the creativity of garden design at its best: the making of a beautiful composition by adding one well-placed ingredient that changes the dynamic completely. The result is a wholly original yet refreshingly simple design.

New Guinea impatiens are ideal for classically shaped designs because they have a compact habit and hold their shape. You can blend white New Guineas with black coral bells and licorice plant to create a dark and gothic composition that remains elegant (photo A).

A (bottom left); B (above)

The more you experiment with juncus, the more interesting it becomes. We found a small container at Southlands Nursery in Vancouver that blended juncus with euphorbia and alternanthera. The sparse euphorbia flutters in between the twining juncus stems like trapped birds, all against a vivid black alternanthera backdrop (photo B).

Coral Dreams

Height: to 20 cm • **Spread:** to 40 cm

WHETHER WE CHOOSE to see it or not, nature is the teacher who never sleeps. When we start to become ingrained in our design habits, its forms and movements never cease to show us how to break out of our ruts. Here, the designer has taken an old concrete bird bath and created a tableau inspired by a thriving coral reef sunken in tropical waters. As a recipe, this piece is impressive, but in its power to convince us to look to the natural world around us for creative design ideas, it is inspiring.

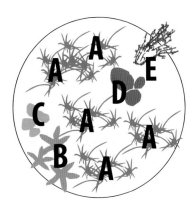

Ⓐ Irish moss

Ⓑ Campanula 'Blue Waterfall'

Ⓒ Sedum

Ⓓ Ajuga

Ⓔ Coral decoration

Recommended container size:
25–40 cm across

The ingredients here couldn't be more ordinary. Irish moss, sedum, ajuga and campanula are all readily available as perennials; often they are the ones overlooked as gardeners rush for the bragging daylilies or black-eyed Susans. The success of the recipe comes from the audacity of blending them together, especially because it goes against many garden design "rules" that we typically follow to create a tableau that is much more than the sum of its parts.

The bird bath, made to look like one-half of an oyster shell, is the perfect container. Its deep swoops and curves emphasize the creeping habit of the ingredients, their stems reaching out as if being swayed by soft currents.

The fan coral backdrop brings a rigid organic architecture to the otherwise rather shapeless composition. If you want to emphasize the coral aspect even more, add some blue-green glass balls that the moss can grow around like seaweed.

This recipe would fit perfectly in any yard with an aquatic theme or even a water fountain or pond. Its small size and delicious attention to detail means that keeping it near your sitting area is a must. It will thrive in partial sun. If it's in full sun you will need to keep it well watered.

'Blue Waterfall' campanula explodes into long strands of cool, star-shaped flowers in late spring.

A Irish moss

Sagina subulata

A long-admired groundcover, Irish moss is always more beautiful close up than people think. While its strictly horizontal shape limits its potential in container gardening, it excels in recipes that emphasize detail over "oompf." In this composition, it fits into its role as a delicate coral seaweed (or possibly anemone) perfectly.

B Campanula 'Blue Waterfall'
Campanula poscharskyana; Serbian bellflower

With scores of calming, star-shaped flowers, this relatively new variety is faster growing and blooms longer than most. While it will still tend to bloom in flushes, as long as it doesn't dry out in the hot sun it will keep going on and off all season.

C Sedum
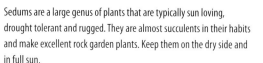
Sedum spp.; stonecrop

Sedums are a large genus of plants that are typically sun loving, drought tolerant and rugged. They are almost succulents in their habits and make excellent rock garden plants. Keep them on the dry side and in full sun.

D Ajuga

Ajuga reptans; bugleweed

Ajuga is a fast-growing perennial that is excellent for designing thanks to its glossy, richly coloured leaves. Its leaves make it ideal for this design. It's invasive, so don't let it near the ground unless you want a long-lasting perennial.

Inspired by Nature

Every garden design is inspired by nature. Without realizing it, we mimic the natural way that plants grow together; we just plant them in smaller, more carefully constructed spaces. When it comes to making beautiful patterns out of living, breathing things, no one does it better than nature, and there is an infinite number of ways to imitate those patterns in our own designs (photo A).

When you set out to design a container that represents nature, like the feature ("Coral Dreams") represents a coral garden, you take mimicking

A (above); B (below)

one step further. Representation is when you strive to create a design that speaks to a specific place/scene in nature. Try not to make your design too literal. Plants aren't oil paints; it's important to walk a fine line between too much abstraction and spelling it out for the viewer. Choose your plants carefully and try to keep additions that spell out what you're representing (like the coral fan in the feature) to a deliberate minimum.

Don't be afraid to represent a specific scene in nature in your designs, and don't be discouraged if it doesn't turn out how you wanted it to (photo B). Representation is one of the more difficult container composition skills because it depends so much on subtlety.

Baby Elephant

Height: to 1 m • **Spread:** to 1 m

THIS RECIPE BLENDS a dark, passionate palette with a compact shape to create a brooding container that pulses with life. Layers of downward sloping leaves and flowers direct the gaze down and into the core of it, mentally lowering its centre of gravity and stabilizing it. The contrasting colours and textures create a dynamic tension that makes it pulse even as it broods, the pillows of flowers pouring out from under watchful colocasia leaves.

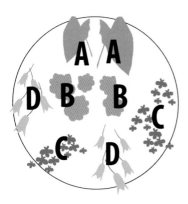

A Colocasia 'Black Magic'

B Impatiens 'Accent Red'

C Lobelia 'Laguna Sky Blue'

D Begonia 'Million Kisses'

Recommended container size:
40–60 cm across

While the shape makes this recipe brooding, contrast makes it dynamic. The pure red flowers and green leaves blaze against each other while the blue lobelia adds variety. As you look closer, you realize that the rounded impatiens blooms contrast with the wickedly sharp begonia flowers flowing beneath.

The colocasia is the perfect centrepiece. Its lines slope downward instead of vaulting upward, pulling the eye down into the flowers below. The matte leaves have a much different effect than the glossy leaves of many other beefy foliage annuals, absorbing the gaze instead of reflecting it. It is the essence of the container; if you were to substitute the colocasia with another big annual, like a red canna lily, the entire mood of the container would change.

This container will perform best if it's protected from the afternoon sun, especially in drier climates. It won't disappoint as an atmospheric centrepiece, brooding in the centre of the garden while everything moves and plays around it. You could also use it in a shady sitting area, or try several containers with identical recipes in a row along a north-facing wall or framing a doorway.

Caladiums are a zesty option for big-leaved containers, but they may be hard to find. Call ahead before you go to the garden centre.

Ⓐ Colocasia 'Black Magic'
Colocasia esculenta; elephant ear, taro

Colocasia is a water plant that is becoming much better known in the container gardening world thanks to recent new varieties. 'Black Magic' boasts bewitchingly black leaves. Keep the soil consistently moist and remember that you can keep the tuber year after year by digging it up in fall and storing it in a clean, dry area over winter.

Ⓑ Impatiens 'Accent Red'
Impatiens walleriana; busy Lizzie

Single impatiens are one of the few old-fashioned annuals that you buy in four- or six-packs that are aggressive enough to compete with much more expensive annuals. Unlike their flashier cousins, the New Guinea impatiens, their matte flowers blend well with the looming colocasia leaves.

Ⓒ Lobelia 'Laguna Sky Blue'
see p. 216

Ⓓ Begonia 'Million Kisses'
see p. 256

Big Leaves for Big Impact

Big leaves have become a staple of large showpiece containers in recent years. Adding big leaves to a container not only gives it an instant modern flair but also makes designing the rest of it simpler. Our eyes are drawn to big, tropical leaves, as if we can subconsciously see the moisture and oxygen they are releasing. When we're intoxicated by gorgeous leaves we're likely to love the whole container and everything else in it.

We found a big-leafed design on the terrace of the Hotel MacDonald that emphasized the vivid contrast of hot pink and ebony black (photo A). The alocasia rises out of the back of the container like a massive palm breaking through the top of the jungle canopy. Below, 'Vista' petunias and black sweet potato vine weave around each other to finish the scene. The filler plants would be an intriguing design on their own, but the alocasia leaves steal the show.

A (above); B (below)

Colocasia is a big-leafed plant that is closely related to alocasia but prefers soil that is more moist. We found a container on an Earl's patio that had giant colocasia leaves unfurling over a bed of brocade geraniums (photo B). Colocasia leaves are just as intoxicating as alocasia leaves and, like alocasia, they steal the show wherever they go!

Sherbet Waterfall

Height: to 1.5 m • **Spread:** to 80 cm

THIS IS THE STYLE of container that I'd expect to find amongst the farmhouses of southern France. It's informal yet carefully designed to bring enough different textures and shapes together to stimulate the eye. The different greens play together to give it a refreshingly cool tone that's sharpened by crisp Mediterranean nasturtium colours.

(A) Phormium 'Yellow Wave'

(B) Rosemary

(C) Nasturtium 'Creamsicle'

Recommended container size:
40–60 cm across

The textures here couldn't be more different. The smooth, lily-pad nasturtium discs layer downward like armour while the erratic, bristling rosemary stems leap out of the pot every way they can. Above all, the long phormium stems arc up and over, defining the space below. It's a deceptively simple mix.

The greens here are so fresh they almost pop right out of the container. Nasturtium leaves boast one of the most refreshing greens of any plant, and combined with the deep, almost forest green of the rosemary and the crisp, cool phormium, they're a monochromatic delight.

This container would be perfect as the centrepiece to a herb or edible garden, perhaps with a number of smaller terracotta pots set around it. The nasturtium flowers are edible (and great as a colourful garnish for salads); just make sure they aren't exposed to any chemicals. This container would also make an excellent centrepiece on its own in the yard;

the large components make it ideal for pulling the eye to a far corner of the garden.

These plants are large and robust, which is what gives this container its appeal. I recommend keeping the phormium year after year if you want to use this recipe to its full potential. Rosemary is also easy to keep year after year, but keep in mind that the woodier it gets the more it tends to lose its sharp flavour, so trim it back hard in spring to encourage newer, tastier growth.

Rosemary is an elegant herb that can be used as a table centrepiece to bring a subtle, soothing scent to the area.

Ⓐ Phormium 'Yellow Wave'
Phormium tenax; New Zealand flax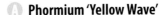

When it comes to grasses, you don't have to be dark to be beautiful. Blonde phormiums bring a cool sense of modernity to recipes and can always be brought inside in fall.

Ⓑ Rosemary
Rosmarinus officinalis

Rosemary has come a long way from its native Sicilian slopes. New varieties are more vigorous and have enhanced flavours for cooking. I recommend 'Tuscan Blue' for containers, as it has the best blend of habit and taste.

Ⓒ Nasturtium 'Creamsicle'
Tropaeolum majus

Nasturtium is a traditional garden classic, but newer varieties for containers grow larger and faster. If you can't find 'Creamsicle,' an older variety such as 'Whirlybird' or 'Alaska' will work; it just may not grow as quickly or have the same Mediterranean palette. Nasturtiums love the sun, and the larger varieties need more fertilizer than others.

The Underappreciated Nasturtium

Nasturtiums are old-fashioned annuals ('Empress of India' is a variety that had its award-winning heyday in 1939) that are starting to be rediscovered as container gardening plants but still have a ways to go. While they have always been gorgeous and full of design potential, a reputation as an old-fashioned rural plant has kept them from breaking into the container gardening mainstream.

One of my favourite features of nasturtiums (besides the fact that the flowers make a great summer salad garnish or gin and tonic garnish) is their vibrant green, disc-shaped leaves. When you're using nasturtiums, think beyond the flower and try to choose container-mates that will provide textural contrast with

A (bottom left); B (above)

the leaves. They are also still one great plant to use along a border because they trail with a lush amount of body and colour (photo A).

Rosemary, like nasturtiums, is beginning to get its well-deserved time in the limelight. Choose your variety carefully because there are many available; I recommend 'Tuscan Blue' for filler plants in containers. Keep it year after year, and it will form a small, exquisitely textured shrub (photo B).

Beneath the Surface

Height: to 25 cm • **Spread:** to 40 cm

GARDENERS ARE JUST starting to realize how easy and versatile succulents are. Their small root systems and resistance to drought make them adaptable to almost any kind of container, even one with very little soil. This recipe uses a shallow pan, seashells and ornamental glass to highlight the blue tones and coral shapes of the echeverias. It's a simple combination that would look exceptional as part of a broader nautical theme (which has become popular in recent years).

Ⓐ Echeveria

Ⓑ Sempervivum

Ⓒ Ornamental glass and seashells

Recommended container size:
30–40 cm across

This recipe is a great example of how simple it is to tell a story just by taking advantage of the colours, textures and shapes of the ingredients. There are so many ways to use the principles of design, and as you start to become more comfortable using and blending them, you'll find yourself getting more and more creative. Practice leads to confidence; confidence is the foundation of creativity.

Three echeverias and a simple sempervivum (any large garden centre will have many to choose from) were all this designer needed to create a container that looks like it could be part of a coral reef. The blue glass draws our eye to the cool blue in the succulent on the right, while the other two echeverias were carefully chosen for their waving leaves and clam-like shapes. The shells (the only actual aquatic prop) finish the scene nicely.

Note the simplicity of the scene here. There are no plastic fish, ceramic fishermen or seahorses to be found. The elements of design speak for themselves.

The echeverias and the sempervivum could be underwater plants, shells or creatures; the subtle sense of abstraction is compelling and keeps us guessing.

Once you start to get comfortable using the basic elements of design, I encourage you to start looking at plants to see what characteristics they have that will allow you to be even more creative. Remember that when you're gardening, especially container gardening, you're creating a living sculpture, and as the artist you have the freedom to play and discover and explore as much as you want.

You can buy ornamental glass in different colours; call around to find the best selection.

🅐 Echeveria

Echeveria spp.; rosette succulent

Once exotic, these plants are becoming easier to find. Ask your local garden centre if there is a well-stocked cactus and succulent section, and you will probably find them there. If you ask for echeveria, you might get a lot of blank looks.

🅑 Sempervivum

Sempervivum tectorum; hens and chicks

There are any number of sempervivums with a variety of colours and textures. If you make the effort to transplant the pups, they also make low-maintenance houseplants or perennials that can be used in containers year after year.

🅒 Ornamental glass and seashells

You can find these at a fish store or even a large garden centre. Often a well-placed prop is the perfect finisher to the story you're trying to tell; just try not to use so many that all the mystery disappears.

Using Decorative Rocks

Using decorative glass or rocks is an easy way to add a whole different personality to your design. In the feature ("Beneath the Surface"), the blue glass is essential to finish the aquatic feel. Glass tends to work best with succulents, but that doesn't mean you shouldn't experiment with other small plants.

A (bottom left); B (above)

Blue-green is a great colour for showcasing the colours of succulents. Green glass is more subtle than bright blue and acts more as a backdrop than an active ingredient. Put it in a container of assorted succulents to help show you just how many different colours and hues there actually are in the design (photo A).

Ornamental glass doesn't always have to be the finishing touch on a representative design (i.e., a container that represents a certain scene in nature, like the feature does). It can be very effective when added just to highlight the colours of the ingredients planted in the container (photo B).

Tut's Treasure

Height: to 1.3 m • **Spread:** to 60 cm

MY MOTHER-IN-LAW designed this showstopper as a centrepiece for her deck containers. It showcases the 'King Tut' papyrus grass by leaving its soaring vertical lines unobstructed so the eye can follow them to the broad whorls above, hovering like palm trees in a desert oasis. Unlike many containers that emphasize downward motion with trailers and vines, this one celebrates upward movement with the 'King Tut' grass and the trachelium.

A Papyrus 'King Tut'

B Trachelium 'Devotion Blue'

C Lobelia 'Laguna Heavenly Lilac'

Recommended container size:
40–55 cm across

Although this container looks like a giant, it actually takes up very little room. Its upward lines are compact, so it would be perfect in the centre of a grouping of close-by containers emphasizing colour, to the effect that, from a distance, the eye is tricked into seeing one large container. The human eye is naturally attracted to straight vertical lines, so while it will work well close to where you like to sit, it will also pull the eye toward it from a distance.

The trachelium mirrors the 'King Tut' grass by branching out in wide blooms, and its rich purple colour adds another layer of interest at the base of the vertical stems. The vivacious lobelia clusters around the trachelium and spills out in every direction, in playful contrast to the stoic stems towering over it. The colours here, purple and lilac, are carefree and full.

'King Tut' needs to be kept moist but also loves a lot of sun, as do the other ingredients here. If you use a terracotta pot, hose it down when you water the plants. Although it can

heat up in the sun, it will also absorb water if kept moist and thus will increase the humidity of the air around it somewhat.

The only drawback to this container is that a central element, the trachelium, tends not to start blooming until midsummer. Before then the lobelia and the 'King Tut' will still look good, but the linking element that makes the recipe cohesive will be missing. If the grass starts to bend and fall over, you may need to either cut off the bent stem or provide a make-shift support with a small peony ring or even garden twine.

Blue trachelium has a rounded, allium-like shape that makes it an eye-catching centrepiece.

Ⓐ Papyrus 'King Tut'

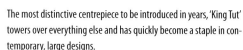

Cyperus papyrus; King Tut grass

The most distinctive centrepiece to be introduced in years, 'King Tut' towers over everything else and has quickly become a staple in contemporary, large designs.

Ⓑ Trachelium 'Devotion Blue'

Trachelium caeruleum; blue throatwort

Trachelium boasts massive colour on broad heads, and when it's in bloom it really catches people's attention. Once the heads are done you can pinch them off, but there probably won't be any more on the way.

Ⓒ Lobelia 'Laguna Heavenly Lilac'

Lobelia erinus; Indian tobacco

Lilac lobelia is the perfect example of how purple can be fun and not just brooding and serious. It's light-hearted, whimsical and easy to grow as long as you give it ample sunlight and fertilizer.

A Different Kind of Grass

'King Tut' is one of the most exciting annuals to come out in years, and it has been quickly taken up by gardeners everywhere who have been looking for a large, easy-to-care-for centrepiece with strong architectural lines.

Use 'King Tut' is you are looking for a grass that is more formal and contemporary than the staple purple fountain grass. It blends well with everything because it has no colours or leaves to harmonize or contrast; it just adds vertical lines so straight that they bring a sense of symmetry no matter where they are (photo A).

Atop these beautiful straight lines are branching plumes that make

A (bottom left); B (above)

a full 'King Tut' feel like a cluster of palm trees towering over a field of flowers below (photo B).

I strongly recommend adding 'King Tut' to one of your designs this season. If you're doubtful of the power that vertical lines have in a design, plant one container with the grass and one without but with the rest of the ingredients identical. Then you'll be able to see for yourself how potent symmetry is in the garden.

Garden of Horrors

Height: to 30 cm · **Spread:** to 20 cm

CARNIVOROUS PLANTS HAVE been around for a long time, but their diminutive size and sometimes complicated care have prevented them from hitting their stride in the container gardening world. Adventurous gardeners who have tried them, however, have usually found them worth the effort. If you have a little extra time to spend in the garden, I urge you to take a chance on these exotic little plants this season.

Ⓐ Venus flytrap

Ⓑ Sarracenia

Ⓒ Lichen branches

Recommended container size:
15–25 cm across

Carnivorous plants work best when their container mimics their habitat. They are small plants, so you will need to pay attention to tiny details as you design. Here, the designer has surrounded the Venus flytraps and the sarracenia with sphagnum moss and branches covered in lichen. These extra elements not only add to the atmospheric appeal by recreating the sense of wild that carnivorous plants take wherever they go, but they also provide a home for tiny flying insects. These insects, which we usually won't notice, are important food for the plants. In effect, this designer has created a tiny ecosystem. This type of setup is perfect for terrariums, as well.

Sphagnum moss is easy to find at a large garden centre, but lichen- or moss-covered branches may be more difficult to find the farther you are from the west coast. Call around to garden centres and high-end flower shops, but if you don't have any luck, curly willow will provide the same gnarled verticality and, if fresh, will root into the soil and sprout leaves.

Please do not go into the bush and steal moss or branches; only buy them from vendors that you trust to be responsible.

Make sure to plant your ingredients into a peat moss–based medium. If you want more carnivorous oddities, call around for sundew, which boasts glistening beads of moisture on its tiny leaves.

Pathiopedilum orchids (tropical lady slippers) can fit nicely into a container with carnivorous plants.

Ⓐ Venus flytrap

Dionaea muscipula

They are always a kids' favourite at the greenhouse, although they often don't end up living very long because they are often fed hamburger or other fatty meats, which are fatal to their very simple digestive system. They need shelter from the sun and a humid environment. The moss will increase the relative humidity, but they will still need to be generously misted daily.

Ⓑ Sarracenia

Sarracenia spp.; pitcher plant

Like most carnivorous plants, sarracenia lives in bogs and as such needs to be kept consistently moist (like the Venus flytrap).

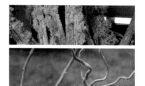

Ⓒ Lichen branches

If you can't find any, try curly willow; see p. 188.

A (above)

Carnivorous Plants in Design

Although carnivorous plants aren't the easiest to take care of, they carry a sense of dark mystery with them that virtually guarantees any design you use them in will be intriguing. Their small size limits them to small, usually minimalist designs, but because they are rarely used in mixed containers, almost anything you do with them will be original.

Take advantage of the unique characteristics of these plants. In photo A, the designer has paired sarracenia, a carnivorous marsh plant, with the contemporary swirls of juncus and some broad, variegated English ivy leaves.

B (above); C (below)

Carnivorous plants are natural partners with all kinds of mosses and
lichens. Lime green lichen on straight
branches provides a sense of vertical
appeal and helps create a sense of
untamed marsh (photo B).

Carnivorous plants have other bene-
fits, as well. Sarracenias are readily
available from large garden centres
and will gobble up their fair share
of mosquitoes if planted in a clump.
Bring them inside in winter because
they aren't frost hardy (photo C).

Frost and Roses

Height: to 45 cm · **Spread:** to 55 cm

SOMETIMES THE JOURNEY from ordinary to extraordinary is so simple that it's easy to overlook. I love this combination because it takes a simple pot of double impatiens (albeit beautiful on their own) and turns it into a dynamic container with both traditional and modern elements. The impatiens rosettes are a classic beauty, and the addition of 'Diamond Frost' euphorbia brings a textural element that modernizes the container while sacrificing none of the original elegance.

A Double impatiens 'Rockapulco Appleblossom'

B Euphorbia 'Diamond Frost'

Recommended container size:
25–40 cm across

The contrasting textures are what make this combination work so well. The 'Diamond Frost' is sharp, clean lines; like frost creeping across a window pane, it creeps amongst the softly curled impatiens blooms.

This recipe uses pink impatiens to emphasize the contrast, but you can use whatever colours you like. Try experimenting with variegated double impatiens or red 'Blush' euphorbia if you want to spice up the combination. Going from soft pink impatiens with white euphorbia to burgundy impatiens with red-tinged euphorbia would make for a very different feel.

Double impatiens like slightly cooler temperatures than their more tropical cousins, New Guinea impatiens. They need to be kept out of the afternoon sun, so the sun-loving euphorbia won't thrive in this container—but that's a good thing. Euphorbia is aggressive in the heat; slowing it down will help keep the balance with its more passive container-mate. Try to keep this one in a sheltered spot, as well. The delicate rosettes are as fragile as they are beautiful, and exposure to strong winds will blow them right off their stems.

I suggest keeping this container close to you. Its classic poise makes it perfect for a sheltered patio where you like to unwind at the end of the day. It is most effective when it's a compact bell shape, so keep the clippers handy. If the impatiens tire in the mid-summer heat, enjoy the euphorbia for a while and keep fertilizing; they should bounce back in early fall.

New Guinea impatiens and heuchera are two plants that work well in a container with a compact shape.

Ⓐ Double impatiens 'Rockapulco Appleblossom'

Impatiens walleriana; rose impatiens, busy Lizzie

Impatiens seem to be a favourite in every region of Canada, with their only drawback being their vulnerability to dry sun and gusty winds. Trim them liberally to keep them from getting leggy.

Ⓑ Euphorbia 'Diamond Frost'

Euphorbia hybrid; diamond frost

The more I travel around Canada, the more places I see this little plant and the more uses there seem to be for it. The variety used here is 'Diamond Frost,' which I find stays the most compact and blooms most fervently. 'Blush' boasts red-tinged leaves and stays so compact that it's really only useful in small- to medium-sized containers.

Using Double Impatiens

Double impatiens keep such a tight bell shape that they are a double-edged sword in designing. Their compact habit is eye-catching, but they keep their shape so well that they tend not to "play" with their other container-mates or grow into an integrated composition. Often double impatiens in a container look like a clump of flowers with the other plants growing around it.

The feature ("Frost and Roses") finds a clever way around this impasse by using a container-mate sparse enough to grow in between the impatiens.

A (bottom left); B (above)

Another trick to use double impatiens in a combination is to plant them with a low-volume trailer so that their bell shape sits on top (photo A).

Double impatiens make a perfect simple and sassy centrepiece for the deck or patio table (photo B). Make sure you put them in a sheltered spot out of direct winds and the afternoon sun. Because they don't trail the pot is very important, especially if they're on a table. I suggest something brightly coloured and fun.

Streams of Gold

Height: to 70 cm · **Spread:** to 50 cm

SOMETIMES YOU JUST have to have a little attitude! This sassy container usually gets a second look. Its use of eye-popping, primary colours along with a mushrooming foliage centrepiece is a unique twist on how we normally design a container. The unexpected centrepiece will make you look twice, and the vibrant colours add the "wow" factor. This one would be perfect in a grouping with smaller, simpler containers that complement the central design.

Ⓐ Coleus 'Dipt in Wine'

Ⓑ Calibrachoa 'Superbells Red'

Ⓒ Mecardonia 'Goldflake'

Recommended container size:
35–50 cm across

The variety of coleus in the container shown is 'Dipt in Wine,' but getting your heart set on a specific variety of coleus often leads to disappointment because there are so many, and no garden centre can carry them all. For this mix, as long as you choose a coleus that's fairly large (check the tag to make sure it grows at least 60 cm tall) and has a pleasing colour scheme, you're in good shape.

You could easily create a crisp triad colour scheme in this design by substituting the centrepiece with a large blue plant such as 'Devotion Blue' trachelium or even a blue Supertunia. Doing so would highlight all three pure, primary colours.

This mix won't really start to pick up steam until June, but once it hits its stride in mid-summer it will be stunning. Mecardonia, though it doesn't bloom until late spring or early summer, stays remarkably compact and crisp as it explodes into bright yellow (while the foliage on many other trailing plants is starting to get leggy).

When you see coleus starting to bloom (it forms a triangle at the top of the branch), nip it off. The blooms distort the shape of the whole plant.

A Coleus 'Dipt in Wine'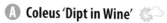
Solenostemon hybrida; flame nettle

Although coleus was traditionally confined to shady spots in the garden, an avalanche of new sun-tolerant varieties means that you can use this foliage staple in any exposure. When you're choosing a plant, make sure it's well branched. If it has only one or two stems when you buy it, that's all it will have all summer unless you pinch it yourself. Give the pot a gentle shake to make sure it has a firm stem and growth habit; a floppy plant indicates unhealthy roots.

B Calibrachoa 'Superbells Red'
Calibrachoa hybrid; million bells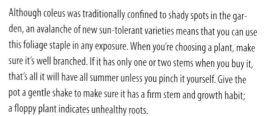

There are a lot of million bells in this book because there's not much they can't do! By mid-summer they will be pouring out from under the coleus leaves and blooming like mad.

C Mecardonia 'Goldflake'
Mecardonia procumbens

'Goldflake' is a relatively new introduction that performs best in warm regions of Canada. It has a dense, compact growth habit with glossy leaves, and although it takes its time blooming, when it does it boasts exceptional colour. By July it will have turned into a sunlight yellow mass of small flowers. Keep it fertilized to maintain its robust habit and the richness in its leaves.

Designing with Coleus

We usually think of coleus as a filler plant, but with its mushrooming habit and full foliage, it can make a beautiful centrepiece. One of the features that makes coleus so useful in design is that, unlike other big foliage plants, which tend to have very glossy leaves, coleus leaves have a matte texture. While the colours are often vivid, the matte finish gives them a softness and a warmth that many contemporary foliage annuals lack.

On the Proven Winners website there is a great example of how coleus can be used as a centrepiece plant (photo A). That designer lined the back of terracotta window boxes with it and had warm, Mediterranean-coloured calibrachoa spilling out. If you're looking

A (above); B (below)

for a foliage centrepiece that won't give your design a contemporary chill, choose a coleus with a warm palette.

I mentioned in my opening paragraph that I would group this container with simpler designs featuring the same ingredients (photo B). If you're thinking of incorporating a design into a larger grouping (and I recommend doing so), remember to keep most of the recipes simple. The complex containers with three or more ingredients should be the culmination of the grouping and not the rule. Too much complexity will overwhelm the viewer.

Doll House

Height: to 30 cm · **Spread:** to 40 cm

THIS ADORABLE CONTAINER uses Mediterranean tones and vivid shapes to create a compact scene almost reminiscent of a school diorama. The soothing, warm hues combine with jagged symmetry to establish an elemental sculpture. The oranges, reds and terracottas throw an intense blast of heat, and the crisp architecture of euphorbia, sedge and moss add an exquisite sense of detail. You will want to keep looking at it, so you might as well keep it in a sunny spot next to where you like to sit.

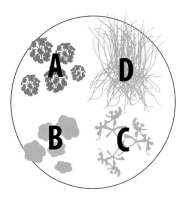

Ⓐ Lantana 'Lucky Red Flame'

Ⓑ Calibrachoa 'Superbells Apricot Punch'

Ⓒ Euphorbia 'Diamond Frost'

Ⓓ Sedge 'Bronco'

Recommended container size:
20–30 cm across

The terracotta pot helps to set a quaint scene here. Its rustic warmth blends perfectly with the soft fires of the calibrachoa and lantana. The sedge adds a sense of nostalgic poise, as it always does, but it's the euphorbia that really brings this container to life. It flutters like a flock of birds lifting off into a prairie sunset.

The moss is long-fibred sphagnum, which is easily found at any large garden centre. It not only hides the black soil but its intriguing form also adds a lot of detail to the composition. Its earthy quality adds to the elemental warmth, though you may have to mist it to keep it green in full sun.

The tiny shapes, especially of the moss and the euphorbia, are my favourite part of this design and the reason that I'd want to keep it close to me. But although the charm of this container is in its compact size, the ingredients aren't typically found in small containers. Many of them can grow very large, but the combination of a small pot and a little pinching will help keep them compact.

If you want to use this recipe but let it grow as large as it wants, you might want to consider a bigger pot or you'll need to keep the watering can handy. Terracotta tends to heat up in the sun and dry out the roots inside it, but fortunately all the plants here can tolerate a little drought.

This simple design uses equally proportioned plants very effectively.

Ⓐ Lantana 'Lucky Red Flame'
Lantana camara; shrub verbena

With some of the most vivid colour in the garden, the only thing stopping lantana from becoming one of the most popular annuals in Canada is its addiction to heat, of which we receive precious little. It also loves humidity and will tend to perform best in hot, humid regions. It has a pungent aroma, so I don't recommend putting it too close to your sitting area.

Ⓑ Calibrachoa 'Superbells Apricot Punch'
Calibrachoa hybrid; million bells

For the million bells in this container, I would stay away from the large Superbells if I was making it again. The Callie Series is a little more compact and may be better behaved.

Ⓒ Euphorbia 'Diamond Frost'
see p. 292

Ⓓ Sedge 'Bronco'
Carex comans; leatherleaf sedge

This rustic-looking grass is perfect for containers that emphasize coarse textures and warm colours. Keep it consistently moist and in full sun to make sure it keeps its rich milk chocolate colour.

Small Scale Designs

Gardens are a place to find a sense of comfort and nurturing, so every garden, no matter how small, should have a place where you can sit back, relax and pass a lazy July afternoon listening to the bees. Small containers can make the perfect final touch for your relaxing spot. While the open spaces are populated with the massive colour of flower beds and large containers, small pots are perfectly contained microcosms of the whole garden at your fingertips.

Often the best plants to use for small containers are small, passive plants such as ferns, but if you want a little more colour, there's nothing wrong with using aggressive annuals. When one plant gets rowdy, simply give it a gentle snip to make it behave. At Southlands Nursery in Vancouver we found a small design using high-performance annuals, and it looked terrific; admittedly, though, in such a small pot it would require a bit more watering once mature (photo A).

A (above); B (below)

Renee Oswald planted a clever blend of aggressive and passive ingredients. She combined the slow-growing polka dot plant *(Hypoestes phyllostachya)* with a more aggressive frosted petunia. The red, white and green in each plant blended together exquisitely, and as the petunia grew larger, the contrast in growth habit and form provided another point of interest (photo B).

Falling Angels

Height: to 1.5 m • **Spread:** to 1 m

I FIRST ENCOUNTERED stories of brugmansia while reading a book by Wade Davis, the brilliant Canadian ethnobotanist. He studies sacred plants, and few plants are as sacred to as many indigenous South American peoples as brugmansia. Native to the cool slopes of the Andes, this close relative of datura has been recently hybridized and is now sought after as a container plant.

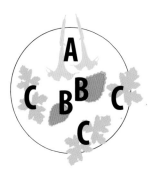

Ⓐ Brugmansia

Ⓑ Coleus

Ⓒ Brocade geranium

Recommended container size:
55–75 cm across

The brugmansia steals the show here, and the coleus, brocade geraniums and calibrachoa below it round out the container. The other ingredients look good, but they are really just there to fill out the unsightly base of the container. They also add a sense of scale that highlights the size of the centrepiece. Substitute freely here; you may want to plant some orange or cream-coloured annuals to harmonize with the star.

This container will thrive in full sun in humid areas; in dry areas it will need partial shade. It can dry out slightly between waterings. "Brugs" smell amazing in the evening, emitting a sweet, potent aroma. Put this one close to where you like to sit after dinner with a glass of wine; you might find the scent as intoxicating as the wine.

You can keep your brugmansia year after year (in about three years it will max out at about 2 metres tall), but be warned that during winter it will lose all its leaves and pout for six months. It responds well to pruning; if you are a savvy pruner you can train

it. It will perform best if the branches are overhanging and as horizontal as possible, like an apple tree. Wear gloves whenever you handle it, and make sure no parts of it come into contact with your eyes or lips.

If you're interested in learning more about the cultural significance of brugmansia, google "brugmansia" or "angel's trumpet," or if you can track down anything by Wade Davis, I highly recommend him.

Me posing with a perfectly pruned brugmansia from Kew Gardens near London, England.

Ⓐ Brugmansia

Brugmansia spp.; angel's trumpet

I'm going to focus on this one ingredient because it is what makes the container. You should be able to find one in a large garden centre; the peach variety is the most common (original) variety and blooms and smells the best. The coloured flowers and variegated leaves may look pretty, but they don't pack the same visual or olfactory punch. **Warning:** all parts of this plant are poisonous and potentially deadly, so if you have small children or pets who like to chew, please choose another ingredient.

Ⓑ Coleus
see p. 296

see p. 296

Ⓒ Brocade geranium
see p. 220

A (above)

More About Brugmansia

While the increasing popularity of brugmansia is making it easier to find, I still recommend calling ahead to a larger garden centre to make sure it's there. Make sure you get a brugmansia; you're likely to get a datura, its smaller cousin, if you ask for angel's trumpet (a common name for both plants).

The peach-coloured brug is the most common, and for good reason. It periodically sends out thick flushes of blooms that can almost cover the tree (photo A). If you're keeping it year after year, prune it as you would an apple tree, promoting horizontal over vertical growth to encourage more flowers.

B (above left); C (above right)

D (below)

The variegated variety (photo B) is sometimes available, but though it's often snatched up for its cream-rimmed leaves, it doesn't bloom as profitably as the more common peach type. Other colours, like pink and red (photo C), usually have to be purchased over the internet to be shipped to you. I've found that the peach not only blooms the most but also has the most intoxicating evening fragrance.

After a few years of overwintering, your brug will become woody and start to resemble a small tree (photo D), which will add yet another element to your designs. The woody trunk will make your designs look old, as if they were planted a decade ago and are now being overgrown by fresh annuals.

Sinister Chandelier

Height: to 60 cm • **Spread:** to 40 cm

THIS RECIPE IS an ideal marriage of a unique container and a unique plant. I included it to demonstrate just how important a role the container can play in your designs. Often we overlook its role as utilitarian and forget that it's just as visible and plays just as large a role in the design as the plants do. People who embrace the potential of containers, like this designer clearly has, enjoy an even broader range of design options that they can use to create their living sculpture.

A Nepenthes

Recommended container size:
30–40 cm across

A container is so much more than just a place to plant your ingredients. It's a part of your creation, and when it comes to the elements of design, the eye doesn't discriminate between the plants and the container. Its colour, its texture, its shape and its proportion to the plants all influence the overall look of the design. You don't necessarily have to go out and buy an expensive container to match your design, though; the more creative you are, the more options you have.

Nepenthes aren't for everybody. They can be hard to find and are tricky to care for, and some people just plain don't like how they look. But people who like nepenthes will love this design because it showcases them at their sleek, cylindrical, alien best. Their pendulous pitchers are one-of-a-kind in the plant kingdom; from a design point of view, they are stunning. When, as a designer, you're confronted with plants with bizarre characteristics, I encourage you to frame your design to showcase, rather than hide, those characteristics.

For a one-of-a-kind plant, this designer has chosen a perfectly simple chandelier, lined it with moss and used it exactly the same as a moss hanging basket. There are even spots for candles. This container would need a very sheltered spot (even morning sun would have to be limited), but in as warm a place as possible. It should never be allowed to dry out and should be misted daily.

Heuchera is ideal for planting in old chandelier frames.

Ⓐ Nepenthes

Nepenthes spp.; pitcher plant

Native to the steamy jungles of Sumatra and Borneo, nepenthes are a carnivorous collectors' item that require high heat, protection from direct sun and very high humidity (a difficult combination in Canada). The species that are available at larger garden centres are typically the easiest to care for, relatively speaking. Nepenthes tend to be a love-it or hate-it plant; I see some interesting facial expressions when gardeners first lay eyes on it in Salisbury.

Showcasing the Bizarre

I'm going to take this chance to talk about some of the more exotic ingredients that are available for the adventurous designer. Unusual plants tend to have small groups of very dedicated admirers who grow, promote and hybridize them, and those groups are often a big reason why the plants stay in circulation. When I have questions about rare plants, I often seek these dedicated

people out and am always amazed at their passion. If you are looking for an unusual plant and can't find it, search online and you will probably run into one of these groups.

Orchid cacti are stunning plants that include the famous 'Queen of the Night' variety (photo A). They are a type of succulent that produces scores of huge, brightly coloured

A (below); B (right)

flowers, and they aren't as hard to grow as many people think.

Some of my favourite unusual plants are in the genus *Tillandsia*, which are air plants in the Bromeliad family. They are epiphytic, meaning they don't like to be planted in soil, and come in a myriad of sizes, textures and shapes. They have a lot of potential for the intrepid designer. Photo B is a picture of a tillandsia tree that I designed for the Devonian Botanic Gardens outside of Edmonton.

The Peacock

Size: depends on design

I KNOW WHAT you're thinking, but no, I'm not suggesting that you turn your yard into a 50-foot peacock. We stumbled upon this stunning showpiece in Minter Gardens, and I'm including it to show you just what's possible with a little space, some extra effort and some creativity. If you're ambitious and want a challenge, creating a living portrait in your garden might be just the thing.

Recommended container size:
depends on design

This is a completely new way of using the elements of design. Instead of using colour and texture to create an abstractly beautiful composition, you're using them to paint a literal picture—in this case a portrait. The key here is not the plants used, but spending a little extra time caring for them so that they keep the shape you need to maintain the overall look.

When you get up close, you see that the peacock's tail isn't made of anything extraordinary. Two types of ageratum (tall and short), lobelia and an outer rim of spirea are all the ingredients this designer needed. The colours blend well together, and the textures have enough body that they express the voluptuous elegance of a peacock's tail. All of these plants love full sun, and they had to be affordable because of the number of them required.

If you're willing to spend some extra effort maintaining it, there's no reason that you can't create a living portrait in your yard. You will need a significant amount of space, room enough for people to be able to stand back and see it properly. Like a mural, it will need to be seen from a distance to be appreciated. Spend some time planning. Sketch it out and mark where each plant is going to go in the ground.

It's important not to be get too ambitious in your design. Note the lack of detail in the peacock's tail. The smaller the detail you try to represent, the harder it will be for you to care for it and for people to see it. The best tools you have are your ingredients, but you'll need to understand their strengths and weaknesses. Their weakness is that they can't convey small details very well (for example, the details of a face unless the portrait is quite large). Their strength is their richness and diversity of colour and texture, which allow the savvy designer to do whatever his or her creativity allows.

Here, the designer at Minter Gardens used blue ageratum and silver-green succulents to great effect.

English ivy

Hedera helix; common ivy

Depending on where you are in Canada, English ivy can be an annual or a perennial. There are dozens of different varieties, each with different shapes or colours of leaves, and they are all very easy to care for and easy to propagate by rooting cuttings in a glass of water. One of the most versatile vines anywhere, it is a staple plant for many designers.

Fibrous begonia

Begonia x *semperflorens-cultorum;* wax begonia

The lady's dress at Minter Gardens is adorned with fibrous begonias. They are old-fashioned annuals that are excellent for living sculptures in the shade because they form a dense mound of colour and don't tend to overgrow. They're available in the green leaf or a bronze leaf type that contrasts with itself.

Milliflora petunia

Petunia x *hybrida*

Another great annual for using in upright garden sculptures is the milliflora petunia. It is the smallest petunia available, often with dime-sized flowers. It produces scores of blooms on well-behaved, mounded plants. Call ahead before you head to the garden centre; the most common varieties are from the Fantasy Series.

Creating Living Sculpture

Living sculptures aren't for everybody, but I wanted to talk about them to show just how many options you have in your flower beds. If the idea of living sculptures has inspired you and you want to create your own, I suggest starting with an English ivy base. English ivy is one of the easiest vines to train on a pre-shaped form (photo A). If you're handy, you can make the form yourself by twisting some heavy wire onto a sturdy frame. It may take a few years for

A (bottom left); B (above)

the ivy to grow in; a living sculpture doesn't happen overnight.

Minter Gardens outside Vancouver has some exceptional examples of living sculptures. The feature ("The Peacock") is the largest, but others are equally as creative. One of their most impressive is an English ivy lady with a flowing fibrous begonia gown (photo B). She stands at a shady resting spot on the path as if waiting for a suitor. Once the English ivy frame was grown and in place, the designer simply had to create an appropriately shaped wire planter to act as the dress.

Glossary

Acid soil: soil with a pH lower than 7.0

Alkaline soil: soil with a pH higher than 7.0

Basal leaves: leaves that form from the crown

Basal rosette: a ring or rings of leaves growing from the crown of a plant at or near ground level; flowering stems of such plants grow separately from the crown

Crown: the part of a plant where the shoots join the roots, at or just below soil level

Cultivar: a cultivated (bred) plant variety with one or more distinct differences from the parent species, e.g., in flower colour, leaf variegation or disease resistance

Damping off: fungal disease causing seedlings to rot at soil level and topple over

Deadhead: to remove spent flowers to maintain a neat appearance and encourage a longer blooming period

Direct sow: to plant seeds straight into the garden, in the location you want the plants to grow

Disbud: to remove some flower buds to improve the size or quality of the remaining ones

Dormancy: a period of plant inactivity, usually during winter or other unfavourable climatic conditions

Double flower: a flower with an unusually large number of petals, often caused by mutation of the stamens into petals

Genus: category of biological classification between the species and family levels; the first word in a scientific name indicates the genus, e.g., *Digitalis* in *Digitalis purpurea*

Hardy: capable of surviving unfavourable conditions, such as cold weather

Humus: decomposed or decomposing organic material in the soil

Hybrid: a plant resulting from natural or human-induced crossbreeding between varieties, species or genera; the hybrid expresses features of each parent plant

Invasive: able to spread aggressively from the planting site and outcompete other plants

Marginal: a plant that grows in shallow water or in consistently moist soil along the edges of ponds and rivers

Neutral soil: soil with a pH of 7.0

Node: the area on a stem from which a leaf or new shoot grows

Offset: a young plantlet that naturally sprouts around the base of the parent plant in some species

pH: a measure of acidity or alkalinity (the lower the pH, the higher the acidity); the pH of soil influences availability of nutrients for plants

Rhizome: a root-like, usually swollen stem that grows horizontally underground, and from which shoots and true roots emerge

Rootball: the root mass and surrounding soil of a container-grown plant or a plant dug out of the ground

Rosette: see Basal rosette

Self-seeding: reproducing by means of seeds without human assistance, so that new plants constantly replace those that die

Semi-hardy: a plant capable of surviving the climatic conditions of a given region if protected

Semi-double flower: a flower with petals that form two or three rings

Single flower: a flower with a single ring of typically four or five petals

Species: the original plant from which a cultivar is derived; the fundamental unit of biological classification, indicated by a two-part scientific name, e.g., *Digitalis purpurea* (*purpurea* is the specific epithet)

Subspecies (subsp.): a naturally occurring, regional form of a species, often isolated from other subspecies but still potentially interfertile with them

Taproot: a root system consisting of one main vertical root with smaller roots branching from it

Tender: incapable of surviving the climatic conditions of a given region; requires protection from frost or cold

True: describes the passing of desirable characteristics from the parent plant to seed-grown offspring; also called breeding true to type

Tuber: a swollen part of a rhizome or root, containing food stores for the plant

Variegation: describes foliage that has more than one colour, often patched or striped or bearing differently coloured leaf margins

Variety (var.): a naturally occurring variant of a species; below the level of subspecies in biological classification; also applied to forms produced in cultivation, which are properly called cultivars

Index

Names in **boldface** refer to designs; page numbers in **boldface** refer to full plant descriptions.

About the Author

ROB HAS BEEN FASCINATED with plants since he was a child. As co-owner of Salisbury Greenhouse just outside of Edmonton, Alberta, he feels privileged to be able to share his passion with gardeners. He especially loves talking to gardeners who are just starting out and are eager to get their fingers dirty. His sense of inspiration is infectious, and he loves getting other people hooked on growing.

In his spare time, Rob writes poetry, climbs mountains in the Rockies, and works toward his Masters of Arts in Literature at the University of Alberta. He lives in Sherwood Park with his beloved wife Meg.